MORE *Free-Motion* Machine Quilting 1-2-3

62 FAST-AND-FUN DESIGNS TO FINISH YOUR QUILTS

D1614340

Lori Kennedy

Martingale®
Create with Confidence

More Free-Motion Machine Quilting 1-2-3:
62 Fast-and-Fun Designs to Finish Your Quilts
© 2018 by Lori Kennedy

Martingale®
19021 120th Ave. NE, Ste. 102
Bothell, WA 98011-9511 USA
ShopMartingale.com

No part of this product may be reproduced in any form, unless otherwise stated, in which case reproduction is limited to the use of the purchaser. The written instructions, photographs, designs, projects, and patterns are intended for the personal, noncommercial use of the retail purchaser and are under federal copyright laws; they are not to be reproduced by any electronic, mechanical, or other means, including informational storage or retrieval systems, for commercial use. Permission is granted to photocopy patterns for the personal use of the retail purchaser. Attention teachers: Martingale encourages you to use this book for teaching, subject to the restrictions stated above.

The information in this book is presented in good faith, but no warranty is given nor results guaranteed. Since Martingale has no control over choice of materials or procedures, the company assumes no responsibility for the use of this information.

Printed in China
23 22 21 20 19 18   8 7 6 5 4 3 2 1

Library of Congress Cataloging-in-Publication Data
Names: Kennedy, Lori, author.
Title: More free-motion machine quilting 1-2-3 : 62 fast-and-fun
    designs to finish your quilts / Lori Kennedy.
Description: Bothell, WA : Martingale, 2018.
Identifiers: LCCN 2017050041 | ISBN 9781604689242
Subjects: LCSH: Machine quilting--Patterns.
Classification: LCC TT835 .K46545 2018 | DDC 746.46--dc23
LC record available at https://lccn.loc.gov/2017050041

MISSION STATEMENT

We empower makers who use fabric and yarn
to make life more enjoyable.

CREDITS

**PUBLISHER AND
CHIEF VISIONARY OFFICER**
Jennifer Erbe Keltner

CONTENT DIRECTOR
Karen Costello Soltys

COVER DESIGNER
Adrienne Smitke

MANAGING EDITOR
Tina Cook

INTERIOR DESIGNER
Regina Girard

ACQUISITIONS EDITOR
Karen M. Burns

PHOTOGRAPHER
Brent Kane

TECHNICAL EDITOR
Nancy Mahoney

ILLUSTRATOR
Sandy Loi

DEDICATION

*To my husband, Tom,
for his steadfast support and sense of humor.*

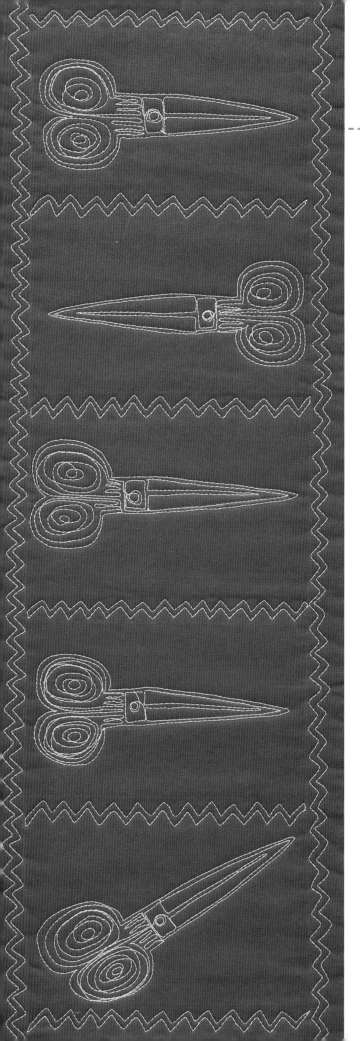

Contents

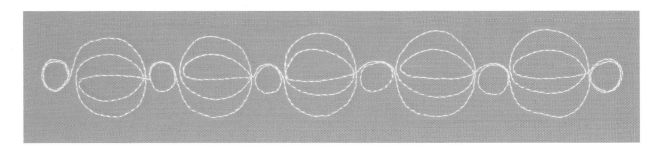

No door is closed to a stubborn scholar.
— Edgar Whitney —

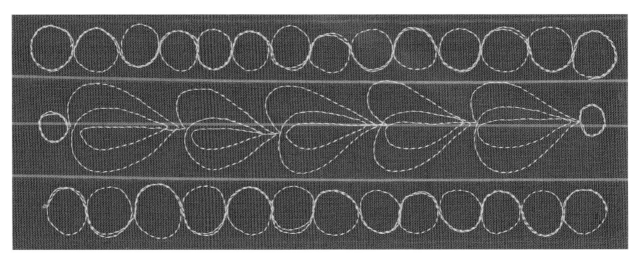

Introduction

Whether you're stitching on an old treadle sewing machine or a modern computerized long-arm model, machine quilting may seem like a daunting process. First, you must overcome your fear of ruining your beautiful quilt top. Next, you need to baste the layers into a quilt sandwich. Finally, you have to figure out a way to fit the huge quilt into that small sewing machine! For many, it's too much to contemplate, so they neatly fold their quilt top into a box and begin another quilt top. Others immediately send their quilt tops off to a professional quilter.

This book is intended to inspire you to overcome your fear of machine quilting so that YOU can make your own custom quilts with personality. There are more than 60 new motifs in this book, including seasonal and holiday patterns to add a festive element to your quilts. Whether you're a beginner or a more advanced quilter, modern or traditional, whimsical or serious, there is a motif for you and your next quilt.

This book is not a comprehensive beginner's quilting guide, however it does offer a wealth of information for all quilting levels. In "Setup and Supplies" on page 6, you'll find information on how to choose the right supplies for your quilting practice, as well as examples of my favorite supplies. In addition, you'll learn how to properly set up your sewing machine to avoid most machine quilting problems, as well as tips for tackling "the Big Quilt."

In "Skillbuilding" on page 15, you'll learn the importance of doodling and discover the Six Essential Doodles every quilter should learn. The Skillbuilding section also includes a variety of small techniques that make a big difference in elevating your machine quilting from good to great.

The best advice I can give you is to be confident! You *can* learn to machine quilt. You can fit your big quilt into that small space. Others have done it…so

can YOU. You must be determined to find a way—but it will have to be your own way. You'll need to find the supplies, thread, needles, and techniques that work for you. Everyone is different and there is more than one way to do any quilting job. The best thing to do is to jump right in and start trying things. Don't wait until you can buy a fancy new sewing machine. Start now. Start with a small quilt and work your way up to larger quilts. Along the way, enjoy the process!

Each challenge results in new lessons learned and each completed quilt brings new confidence. Each motif stitched into a quilt adds to the workbasket of patterns you can use forever, and each quilt is a building block for bigger and better quilts. Don't worry that you will "ruin your quilt with your quilting." You probably will stitch a few quilts that don't live up to your own expectations. Chalk it up to your education and move on! In other words, give yourself permission to fail. It's part of the process.

Allow plenty of time to complete each project. Short deadlines are the thief of quilting joy. Take your time as you stitch samples, doodle, plan, make mistakes, and try new things.

Make the process fun by choosing fabric, thread, and motifs you LOVE. Select quilting motifs that reflect your personality or the recipient's personality. Entertain yourself by stitching hidden messages, jokes, Bible verses, or song lyrics into the quilted lines.

When you finish the last stitch, you'll have created a truly custom quilt—one that cannot be purchased from a store or designed with a pantograph. Your quilt will be a work of art. It may not be "perfect"—it will be even better! Your quilt will be like a handwritten letter to your friends, family, and future generations. May your quilt be a love letter!

Happy Stitching!
xxx *Lori* xxx

Setup and Supplies

Once the quilt top is finished, it's time to transform it into a quilt with the magic of machine quilting. There are a few simple steps to take before the quilting can begin: set up your sewing machine for free-motion work, choose batting, layer and baste the quilt sandwich, select thread, and plan your quilting design. The steps are simple but important in determining the final look and feel of your quilt masterpiece.

Setting Up Your Machine

The best sewing machine on which to begin free-motion quilting is the one you own right now. Whether your machine is old or new, treadle or computerized, it can be adapted to free-motion quilting.

On page 7 is "The 12-Step Setup," a quick guide to preparing your machine for quilting. Following the steps will allow your quilt to move easily, without interference from the feed dogs, so that you can create the best-looking stitch possible. By carefully walking through each step, you can avoid most common machine quilting problems. I recommend making a copy of the list and taping it to your sewing table for ready reference. When you need help performing a step, refer to the explanations that follow and to your sewing-machine manual.

Step 1: Clean and Oil Your Machine

Begin each free-motion quilt project by cleaning and oiling your sewing machine. Broken threads in the bobbin case can lead to tension problems, and lint buildup will hinder proper stitch formation. Due to the fast sewing speed and fibers migrating from the batting layer, free-motion quilting leads to more lint buildup and requires more frequent cleaning and oiling than other types of sewing.

Step 2: Thread the Bobbin

Once the machine has been cleaned and oiled, wind several bobbins and thread the bobbin case as for normal sewing. If the bobbin requires a tension adjustment, do it only after stitching a sample and adjusting the top tension (step 11 on page 8).

Step 3: Attach a Straight-Stitch Plate

The stitch plate is the metal plate that sits below the needle and presser foot. It has an open area for the feed dogs and a hole for the needle to pass into the bobbin area. Many sewing machines come with two stitch plates: a zigzag plate and a straight-stitch plate. The zigzag plate has a wide opening, allowing the needle to move back and forth as it creates zigzags and other decorative patterns. It may be as wide as 9 mm. The straight-stitch plate, also called a single-hole throat plate, has a single hole for straight stitching and provides more support to the fabric as the needle penetrates the quilt, preventing the fabric from being pushed into the needle opening, which in turn allows for better stitch formation.

Engage Safety Feature

If your machine has a safety icon or button for the type of stitch plate you're using, engage it now. It will prevent you from switching to a zigzag setting later, which can save you from breaking your needle!

Step 4: Attach a Table Extension

In order to free-motion quilt smoothly, it's important to provide as much support for the quilt as possible. The completely flat surface provided by a set-in sewing cabinet is ideal. Extension tables, such as the Sew-Steady table from Dream World Northwest, are a good alternative and are available for most sewing-machine models. Alternatively, boxes or phone books can be placed level with the sewing-machine bed to create a wider sewing surface to support the quilt. For very large quilts, add an ironing board or a banquet table beside the sewing machine to support the weight of the quilt.

Step 5: Tape a Supreme Slider in Place

The Supreme Slider by LaPierre Studio is a Teflon sheet that adheres to the sewing bed and reduces friction during free-motion quilting. The Supreme Slider has a self-sticking back; however, to avoid accidentally stitching the Supreme Slider into the quilt if it shifts during quilting, many quilters use painter's tape to hold the sheet in place. The Supreme Slider is an optional accessory, but one of the few I highly recommend.

Step 6: Insert a New Needle

To ensure the best stitch formation, always begin a quilt project with a new needle. During free-motion quilting, the needle passes through the fabric hundreds of times per minute. In addition, free-motion quilting often creates a slight tug on the needle as the quilt is maneuvered. Change your needle whenever you see skipped stitches, notice tension changes, or detect a change in the sound of your machine—all indicators that the needle is dull or bent. Because of the precision needed to create a perfect lockstitch (formed when the needle passes into the bobbin), even the slightest damage to the needle will lead to improper stitch formation.

Needle type. Sharp needles (as opposed to ballpoint needles) work best for free-motion quilting and are available as quilting, Microtex, jeans, and topstitch needles. A topstitch Sharp needle is my favorite because it has an extra-long eye, a deep groove in the blade of the needle that cradles the thread, and a sharp point.

Needle size. The size of the needle is determined by the weight of the thread. Heavier threads (smaller number) require a needle with a larger eye. A rule of thumb is to pair 50-weight thread with a size 80/12

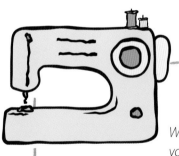

The 12-Step Setup

While the list may seem long, you'll be able to perform all of these steps quickly and start free-motion quilting in less than five minutes.

1. *Clean and oil your machine.*
2. *Thread the bobbin.*
3. *Attach a straight-stitch plate.*
4. *Attach a table extension.*
5. *Tape a Supreme Slider in place (optional).*
6. *Insert a new needle.*
7. *Attach a free-motion quilting foot.*
8. *Disengage the feed dogs.*
9. *Activate the needle-down function.*
10. *Thread the machine.*
11. *Stitch a test sample and adjust tension.*
12. *Begin stitching!*

needle. Increase the needle size to 90/14 for 30- and 40-weight threads and decrease the size of the needle to 70/10 for finer 60-weight thread. Skipped stitches and frayed or broken thread may indicate that the needle is the wrong size for the thread you're using.

Titanium Needles

Needles coated with an ultra-thin layer of titanium stay sharper up to six times longer than standard needles.

Step 7: Attach a Free-Motion Quilting Foot

Depending on the make and model of your sewing machine, you may have a choice of several presser feet for free-motion quilting. The appropriate foot is often called a darning foot, but choose the option that provides the greatest visibility. I like an open-toe foot with an offset shank.

Step 8: Disengage the Feed Dogs

In normal sewing, the feed dogs advance the fabric with every stitch. In free-motion quilting, the quilter controls the speed and direction of the quilt without interference from the feed dogs. On most sewing machines the feed dogs can be lowered to disengage their function by switching a button. Alternatively, set the stitch length to zero and the feed dogs will remain in the original position but won't advance the fabric with each stitch.

Step 9: Activate Needle Down

Many modern sewing machines offer a "needle-down" option. When you use this function, every time you stop sewing the needle ends in the down position in the fabric. Engaging the needle-down function is very helpful in free-motion quilting, allowing you to maintain a continuous line of stitching when stopping to adjust quilt position or hand position.

Step 10: Thread the Machine

With the presser foot in the up position, to properly engage the tension discs, thread the top of the machine as for normal sewing. For the best thread choices, see "Thread" on page 11.

Step 11: Stitch a Test Sample and Adjust Tension

Whenever starting a new project, stitch a sample to test tension, thread color, and the quilting motif. Most sewing machines have factory-set tensions suitable for straight stitching on two layers of fabric. Because free-motion quilting involves three layers, disengaged feed dogs, and a variety of thread types, it's likely that you'll need to make tension adjustments. Always adjust the top thread tension before making any bobbin adjustments. Tension adjustments may be required for each project, and on each day, because factors such as thread, batting, needle, and humidity all affect tension. For more on adjusting tension, see page 21.

Step 12: Begin Stitching!

Once the tension is adjusted and the stitches look perfect on your sample, you're ready to quilt.

The Quilt Sandwich

The quilt sandwich consists of three layers: the quilt top, batting, and backing fabric. The top layer should be pressed, and may be marked, before layering. Likewise, before layering, the batting layer may be soaked or unfolded and left open to rest, allowing the fibers to relax. The backing should be pressed. I also like to starch the backing, as that makes it easier to slide along the sewing table. The layers are secured with pins or spray basted so that the machine quilting fun can begin! Details on each step follow.

PREPARING THE QUILT TOP

To prepare the quilt top for quilting, press it well. It's very difficult to remove wrinkles once the quilting is complete, and quilting stitches look best on a well-pressed quilt top. Many quilters also starch the quilt top to give it a smoother finish and to make marking easier. If you use starch, you may need to wash your quilt after it's completed to remove the starch. If you plan to mark the quilt top, now is the time (see "Design Considerations" on page 28). Use yardsticks, rulers, and/or stencils to divide large quilt blocks and borders into smaller, easier-to-design sections. For example, divide a wide border into 6" sections for quilting the Perfect Pumpkin (page 102). Or, divide large squares into two triangles when stitching the Spiderweb (page 94). Add detailed marks, like tick marks for spacing motifs, once the quilt is layered and stitching is in progress.

A variety of my favorite marking tools

A Note about Quilting Supplies

A daunting number of supplies designed to make free-motion quilting easier are available. Searching for the next best idea and testing every possibility can prevent you from making progress when learning how to free-motion quilt. Acquire gadgets slowly and only in response to a difficulty. If something is not working for you, then seek out possible remedies. Develop your own favorites and your own work style based on the materials, supplies, and styles YOU like best.

MARKING TOOLS

A few simple tools are all you need to mark a quilt top for free-motion quilting.

Rulers

You'll find a wide variety of rulers available for quilters. Use shaped rulers like triangles, diamonds, circles, and squares to subdivide quilt blocks and maintain variety in your free-motion quilt patterns. In addition to rulers designed for quilters, search for interesting rulers and stencils in office-supply and art stores.

Stencils

Stencils provide a great way to create complex patterns made up of a variety of motifs. Use a stencil when the motif is too complex to doodle or memorize easily. Grid stencils are available in a variety of widths and are particularly useful for free-motion quilting grid designs.

Quilt Marking Tip

Some pen marks are removed by ironing and others are permanently set by ironing. Be sure to follow the manufacturer's instructions. If you plan to spray baste your quilt and iron the layers, use marking pens only after the quilt sandwich has been basted.

Marking Pens

You'll use different marking methods for different quilting applications. Light and dark fabrics require different marking tools as well. Look for pens that:

- ✘ Are easy to see
- ✘ Are easy to erase
- ✘ Don't break readily
- ✘ Don't dry out quickly

A few marking tools I use include:

Mechanical ceramic pencils. These are available from Fons and Porter and Sewline in dark and white. The ceramic lead creates a fine line that is easy to erase with a white eraser or damp cloth.

Chalk cartridge set. This set has exchangeable colored chalks in a penlike cartridge, from Dritz Quilting. The chalk line is relatively thick, easy to see, and easy to erase with a microfiber cloth.

Chaco liner. This rolling wheel marker by Clover lays down a thin line of powder. It works well for straight lines or with grid stencils and brushes off easily. It's available in several colors and is refillable.

FriXion pen. This pen, by Pilot, is favored by many award-winning quilters because it creates a very fine line that is easy to see. The ink erases with a burst of steam. A faint residue line remains and the line may reappear when the fabric gets cold unless the quilt is washed with a special ink-removing cleaner, such as Amodex or Motsenbocker's Lift Off No. 3.

Test! Test! Test!

Create samples of your marking tools on the fabrics used in your quilt. Be sure you are able to remove the markings before using on your finished quilt top. Use a light touch with all marking pens and remove the lines as soon as possible.

BATTING

Batting is available in different fibers: cotton, wool, polyester, bamboo, and silk. Each fiber has unique characteristics. When choosing batting for your free-motion quilt projects, consider the following.

How far apart can the quilting lines be placed? Stitch-distance recommendations are listed by the manufacturer on the packaging. You can stitch closer than the recommended spacing, but if the stitches are farther apart the batting will clump inside the layers after washing.

Does the fiber breathe? Polyester fibers do not allow as much airflow as cotton and wool. Some people find polyester less comfortable in quilts used on beds.

Does the fiber have memory? Some fibers, such as wool and polyester, have the ability to relax after folding and are more crease-resistant than other battings.

Does the fiber have loft? Polyester and wool battings are known for their ability to "bounce" up and fill the area between stitching lines. Depending on your project, this quality may or may not be desired.

Does the batting beard? Polyester and wool batting fibers may migrate through the quilt top or backing and become visible on the surface of the quilt. Use batting that has a scrim or that has been bonded to resist bearding. To minimize the effect of bearding, choose a batting color—gray, black, or white—that most closely matches your quilt.

Can I layer or combine two battings? Most manufacturers offer battings that are blends of two fibers, to take advantage of their unique qualities. Some quilters create their own batting blends to suit their needs. For example, you might layer cotton (for its smooth drape) with wool (for its crease resistance). Or you could use two layers of cotton for more loft.

Is preshrinking necessary? Because all batting—including polyester—can shrink, some quilters soak batting before layering it into a quilt. Preshrinking batting ensures that the finished quilt will look the same both before and after being washed. Other quilters prefer the slightly textured look that results when the batting shrinks during laundering; therefore, they don't soak the batting before quilting. Read the batting manufacturer's instructions and create samples to determine which method works best for each of your quilts.

Will the batting color show through? If your quilt contains large areas of very light or white fabric, choose bleached batting. If your quilt is very dark, use a black or gray batting to minimize the visibility of fibers that migrate to the top of the quilt or are loose during the quilting process.

THE BACKING FABRIC

Good-quality cotton fabric is the best choice for backing. If possible, avoid tightly woven fabrics like batiks and bed sheets. Tightly woven fabrics are more difficult for the needle to penetrate and may result in tension and stitch-formation challenges. For the same reasons, avoid fabrics that are painted or that have a surface texture applied, such as some white-on-white fabrics.

Avoid using unwanted, old fabric on the back of a quilt. It's tempting to use our not-so-loved fabrics this way, thinking no one will ever see them. However, the backs of quilts are frequently noticed when a quilt is used. Use good-quality fabrics in colors and patterns that complement the quilt top. The back of the quilt is a design opportunity!

Prints conceal, solids reveal. Choose solid fabric or small-scale prints if you'd like to see the quilting on the back of the quilt. If you prefer a subtle, textured effect, use prints for the backing. Always press the backing carefully before basting the layers. Wrinkles in the backing are very difficult to remove once the quilt has been quilted. Apply spray starch on the right side of the backing fabric to help it slide easily on the sewing table.

Layering and Basting

Once the top, batting, and backing layers have been prepared, baste the layers together using basting spray or safety pins. To keep the layers smooth, use office-supply binders (or tape) to secure the backing, right side *down*, to a table. Next, center the batting layer over the backing. Starting from the center and working toward the edges, smooth out the batting and clamp the two layers to the table. Finally, position the quilt top, right side *up*, on the batting layer. Smooth the quilt top and clamp all three layers. Starting in the center, use small safety pins (size 1) to pin the quilt approximately every 6".

Another option is to use basting spray. Follow the manufacturer's instructions and allow the quilt ample time to dry before quilting to prevent adhesive residue from gumming up the sewing-machine needle and creating stitching problems.

Quilting thread is available in a variety of fibers and weights.

Thread

Choosing thread is one of the most rewarding aspects of free-motion quilting. High-quality thread is available in a vast array of fibers, colors, weights, textures, and sheens. The right thread will make your quilting look better instantly. When choosing thread, the primary design consideration is whether you want the quilting to be highlighted or to serve as a subtle background texture. Keep in mind that different areas within a single quilt will likely have different design needs. In other words, there may be areas of the quilt where you want the quilting to be highlighted and other areas where you want to feature appliqué or piecing instead, with the quilting providing a background texture. Choose the fiber, weight, sheen, and color of thread based on the following design choice: reveal or conceal.

THREAD FIBER

Quilting thread is available in many fiber types. Each fiber has a characteristic look and hand. Common fibers used for quilting thread include cotton, rayon, polyester, silk, metallic, and monofilament.

Cotton thread comes in three quality levels determined by the length of the staple used to create it. Extra Long Staple (ELS) cotton is the highest quality; Long Staple (LS) is also very good. Spools that are not ELS or LS are the lowest grade. Choose ELS or LS cotton for best results when machine quilting.

Rayon thread is known for high luster or sheen. It doesn't have the high tensile strength of other fibers and consequently is not used in quilt construction; however, the strength is more than sufficient for machine quilting. Rayon is not always colorfast, so you may want to avoid it for quilts that require heavy laundering.

Polyester thread is known for its high sheen, though it can also have a duller finish. Polyester is low lint and withstands bleaching, and so may be used for any quilt. Trilobal polyester threads have a high sheen, come in a wide variety of colors, and are a nice option for machine quilting both bed and art quilts.

Silk thread is known for beautiful sheen, color, and smoothness. Silk threads are available in many weights and can be used to create either subtle texture within a quilt or prominent areas of quilting. Silk is a gorgeous fiber; however, it's the most expensive to manufacture.

Monofilament, or invisible thread, is used to create texture only, with the minimum of visible stitching lines. Monofilament is very fine and is available in both polyester and nylon fibers. Choose a monofilament that is soft and pliable. Many quilters use monofilament for allover quilt designs when the goal is to blend with many fabric colors and prints.

Four Threads for Every Quilt

Most quilts require several types of thread for a variety of machine quilting tasks: stabilizing, focus, texture, and bobbin. Consider the fiber, weight, and color when choosing the right thread for each task.

Stabilizing thread. *Used to stabilize the quilt at the beginning of quilting, this thread should be lightweight and blend with most of the fabrics in the quilt.*

Focus thread. *When you are stitching an elaborate motif and you really want it to show, choose a heavyweight thread of a contrasting color. Several color choices may be necessary in different areas of the quilt.*

Texture thread. *Choose a lightweight thread in colors that match the quilt when you want the quilting line to be in the background and create texture only. Consider using several colors of threads in different areas of the quilt to maintain the "texture only" effect.*

Bobbin thread. *A lightweight thread in the bobbin will keep you stitching longer with fewer always-frustrating "empty bobbin" breaks. If your tension is not perfect, consider changing your bobbin thread color every time you change the top thread color.*

THREAD WEIGHT, SHEEN, AND COLOR

Thread-weight classifications can be confusing. Not only are there three different weight systems in use today (tex, denier, and weight), each manufacturer measures differently. To add to the confusion, thread weight gets *heavier* as the number gets *smaller*.

When choosing thread, remember that weight and thickness are relative terms. A 50-weight thread is finer than a 30-weight thread, but don't expect two 50-weight threads from different manufacturers to look or feel the same.

Choose a lightweight thread (50 or 60 weight) whenever you want the quilting line to form a subtle texture. Choose a heavier-weight thread (40 or 30 weight) when you want the quilting motif highlighted within the design.

The *sheen* of a thread refers to the fiber's ability to reflect light. The level of sheen is a design choice and a matter of preference. If the design requires a subtle texture, choose a low-sheen thread.

Thread is available in a vast array of colors. When you want the stitching line to blend, choose a thread that matches the fabric. When you want the quilting line to be more visible, choose thread that contrasts with the fabric.

Variegated threads are another great option for machine quilting. Spool off several inches of thread and let it pool on top of your quilt to see how the colors blend. Be aware that if the variegated thread includes colors that match the fabric, the quilting line will disappear and any quilted motif will look incomplete. Test the thread throughout the quilt to ensure that the colors within the thread provide the design qualities you seek.

SAMPLING THREADS

Before quilting any project, spend a little time testing thread options. Choose several spools of thread in different weights, fibers, and colors. Spool off several inches of thread and let it pool directly on the quilt. Check the color and sheen. Once you've narrowed down the choices, stitch samples of each thread on leftover quilt fabric or on a spare block. Consider using several threads within a single quilt.

Take the time to sample threads on fabric from your quilt. Quilting is more visible on solid fabrics than on prints, so save the most elaborate quilting for less patterned areas.

BOBBIN THREAD

My favorite bobbin thread is Aurifil 50-weight cotton. It's lightweight, medium sheen, and slightly textured, which helps the sewing machine lockstitch with top threads that are often more slippery.

Fiber. Cotton, polyester, and monofilament fibers all have sufficient strength and texture to use in the bobbin. While I frequently use rayon thread on the top, I avoid using it in the bobbin. Rayon is too slippery to create a good lockstitch or knot, especially when combined with rayon or other slippery thread on top.

Weight. For best tension results when machine quilting, choose a bobbin thread that is the same or a lighter weight than the top thread. Matching or decreasing the weight helps the top thread win the tension tug-of-war and keeps the bobbin thread on the back of the quilt.

Color. For the best-looking stitch, match the bobbin color to the top thread. Matching the color hides any slight imperfection in tension.

Sheen. Any level of sheen is appropriate for the bobbin thread.

Try This!

For a subtle, hand-stitched look, choose a bobbin thread color a shade darker than the quilt fabric and tighten the top tension slightly. This will pull the bobbin thread to the top and add emphasis to the points between each stitch.

Planning Quilting Designs

Once the machine is set up, the quilt sandwich prepared, and the thread chosen, the quilting begins! While machine quilting is quicker than hand quilting, it is not quick. With each quilt, allow yourself enough time to plan and design quilting that will enhance the piecing and appliqué on the quilt top. Browse the Internet to see how other quilters have quilted your quilt pattern. Test several motifs using "essential doodling" techniques (see "Skillbuilding" on page 15). Divide the quilt into sections and use motifs to enhance each block, sash, corner square, and

border instead of using a single motif over the entire quilt just to get it finished. You don't need to design every inch of the quilt before you start quilting. Instead, choose a few motifs to start and let the quilt speak to you as you progress.

Creating Samples

Take the time to create samples of batting, threads, and motifs. Use leftover fabric or blocks from the quilt top, as well as the same backing fabric, to get an accurate view of how the quilting will look in your finished quilt. Try several battings. Check weight, loft, and drape. Once you've chosen the batting, use it to create test sandwiches for thread samples. Test thread on different fabrics within the quilt. Can you find a single thread color that will accomplish your design goals throughout the quilt? Or will you need to change threads to create different effects within the quilt? Can you create "The Perfect Stitch" (page 20) with the chosen top and bobbin thread? Once you've selected the thread and batting, test a few motifs. Try quilting designs and combinations of motifs, as well as testing the scale of each motif. Finally, allow yourself the time to practice free-motion quilting. It's a skill that takes time to perfect!

Test threads, batting, and motifs in small wholecloth quilts. Add a binding and enjoy your little quilt. See more in "Gallery" on page 140.

Skillbuilding

Goal setting is the key to skillbuilding. Instead of fretting about your less-than-perfect machine quilting, enjoy the process and strive for progress. With each quilt, try a few new motifs and concentrate on improving one technique. Every quilt will then be a building block to mastery. Some skills, like quilt design, progress over a lifetime. Other techniques, like understanding stopping points, can be learned more quickly.

Doodling

One of the fastest ways to improve your machine quilting is through doodling. Doodling helps develop muscle memory for each motif, but it also does much more. Regular doodling practice helps you develop a natural movement pattern, allowing you to create smooth lines and improve your ability to space by eye rather than by marking.

Six Essential Doodles

Just a few lines form the building blocks of a wide variety of quilting motifs. The Essential Doodles include four simple lines along with circles and spirals. If you practice these doodles regularly, your quilting will improve quickly and learning new motifs will be easier.

Doodle each of the basic lines as well as the mirror-image line. Use lined paper or graph paper and try different widths and spacing for each of the Essential Doodles. Doodle the line from top to bottom and then from bottom to top. Practice the line from left to right and then reverse and doodle from right to left. Repeat each line by "echo doodling" and combine the lines to create patterns. Keep doodling until the line becomes a natural part of your movement pattern just like handwriting. Eventually each line will have your signature.

THE SWEEP

The Sweep begins on one line and gently curves to another line.

Use this doodle to make the Candy Cane Border (page 39), Lovely Carnation (page 56), and Braided Wheat (page 88).

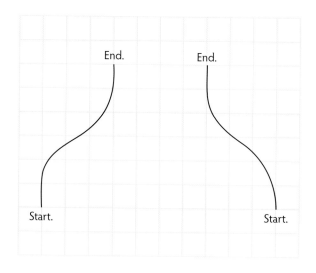

THE TAPERED SCALLOP

The Tapered Scallop begins on one line, tapers into a scallop, and then tapers back onto the same line.

Use this doodle to make the Japanese Lantern (page 90) and Ribbons (page 104).

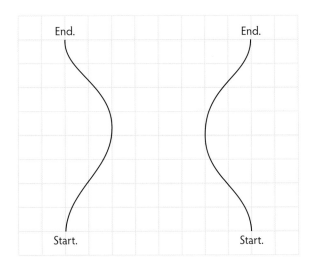

THE S CURVE

The S Curve begins and ends on the same line and is a shallow version of the letter "S". It's created by smoothly connecting a Tapered Scallop and a mirror-image Tapered Scallop.

Use this doodle to make the Honeycomb (page 134), Hostas (page 64), and the centerline of many vine motifs.

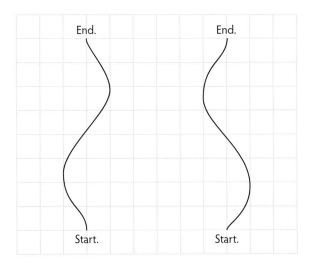

THE CURL

The Curl is a wavy line with a rounded top. It forms the center of many flowers and can be added as a flourish to other motifs.

Use this doodle to make the Perfect Poinsettia (page 38), Easy Breezy Flower (page 72), and the Classic Marigold (page 80).

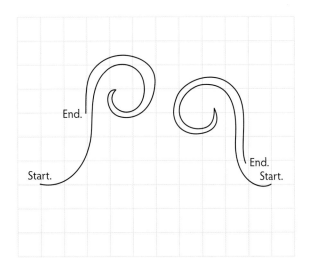

CIRCLES

Learn to doodle both clockwise and counterclockwise circles. For quilting purposes, each circle is 1½ revolutions. By combining the two directions, it's easier to develop a doodling and quilting rhythm. Doodle rows of circles from very small to large. Try filling a page of paper quickly with both clockwise and counterclockwise circles.

Use this doodle to make the Perfect Poinsettia (page 38) and Sticks and Stones (page 127).

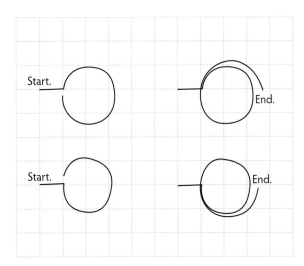

SPIRALS

You can doodle a spiral several ways, and any version can be substituted in the quilted motifs. Develop your clockwise and counterclockwise rhythm by starting with Messy Spirals and work your way up to Basic Spirals.

Messy Spirals

Doodle Messy Spirals by spiraling clockwise in toward the center of a circle and counterclockwise out toward the edge. Do not worry about the spacing between the rows.

Use this doodle to make the Sewing Scissors (page 114) and Circus Train (page 122).

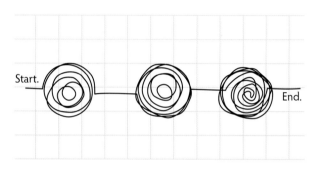

Silly Spirals

Begin with a short line and doodle rows of clockwise or counterclockwise spirals. Make them large and small. Work on creating even spacing between rows. Be sure to learn both clockwise and counterclockwise versions.

Use this doodle to make the Silly Spiral Flower (page 52), Silly Spirals (page 126), and Loose Screws (page 128).

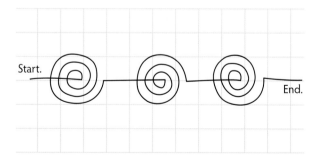

Basic Spirals

The Basic Spiral is created by doodling clockwise in to the center and counterclockwise out from the center with even spacing. The Reverse Basic Spiral is created starting counterclockwise and finishing clockwise in one smooth line. When doodling or stitching the Basic Spirals, slow down to get the spacing just right. You can find more about Spirals in *Free-Motion Machine Quilting 1-2-3* (Martingale, 2017).

Use this doodle to make the Windowsill Garden (page 78) and Sewing Scissors (page 114).

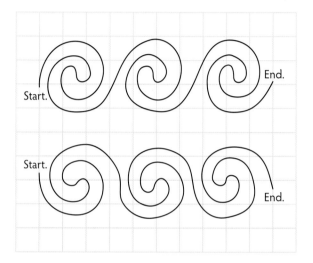

Doodling and Quilt Design

Before you begin stitching motifs onto your quilt, spend time doodling the motifs. Choose a few motifs and doodle them to be sure you're comfortable with the stitching order. Draw sample blocks and doodle the motifs to check for good contrast and scale, and then doodle the motifs to determine the best way to travel between motifs and blocks.

LEARNING A NEW MOTIF

Whenever you learn a new motif, it's best to doodle it many times until you can doodle it without hesitation. Repetition develops the muscle memory required to machine quilt the pattern smoothly, without any of the stutter stitches that occur when you hesitate even for a moment. Doodling a new design 50 to 100 times may take only a few minutes and will improve your quilting significantly. Once you're comfortable doodling the motif, doodle it on a note card or add it to a notebook for future reference. Stitch a sample of the motif as well.

PLANNING MOTIFS FOR A QUILT

When choosing the motifs for a quilt, draw the block shapes or borders onto a piece of paper or into a notebook, and use tracing-paper overlays to sample potential motifs. Alternatively, place the piece of paper with the quilt shapes into a clear vinyl or plastic folder or sheet protector and use dry-erase markers to sample motifs. Allow yourself enough time to sample many options and combinations. Taking the time to audition quilting motifs can transform a good quilt into a great quilt.

DETERMINING THE SCALE OF A MOTIF

Once you've chosen the motifs for your quilt, practice doodling each of them in the sizes that best suit your quilt. Some motifs can simply be stitched as shown but at a larger scale, while others look best if the size is increased by adding layers or by adding echo stitching. Remember to keep each motif's scale small enough that maneuvering the quilt to stitch it doesn't become a burden.

PLANNING TRAVEL STITCHING

Spend some doodling time determining the best way to move from one motif to another and from one block to another. Travel stitching may be done by overstitching a previous stitching line, stitching in the ditch of a seamline, or by creating a connecting line, such as a loopy line between motifs. Consider the weight of the thread you're using. When using a fine-weight thread, it's easy to hide travel stitching by stitching in the ditch or by overstitching. When using a heavyweight thread, overstitching can create an undesirable line that is harder to camouflage, and it might be better to knot off. These decisions are easier to make during planned doodling.

In motifs like Dog Bones (page 120), travel stitch by adding a loopy line between the motifs.

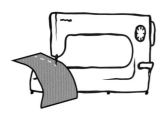

The Perfect Stitch

Creating beautiful stitches is the most important step in achieving high-quality quilting. The *perfect stitch* is balanced and even, with each stitch visible, and will likely require some machine adjustment to attain. Perfect stitch formation is more important than replicating each motif perfectly. For example, a perfectly round spiral will look terrible if the tension is too tight, whereas a row of imperfectly shaped circles will still look nice if the stitch created by the machine looks great.

Many of the steps in "The 12-Step Setup" (page 7) are designed to help you achieve the perfect-looking stitch. Cleaning and oiling your machine, using a straight-stitch plate, choosing the right top and bobbin threads, and learning how to adjust your tension are essential to creating the perfect stitch.

Balanced Tension

The perfect stitch should be balanced between the top and bobbin threads. In other words, the bobbin thread shouldn't show on the top of the quilt, and the top thread shouldn't show on the back of the quilt. It's almost impossible for any sewing machine to create perfect balance at all times when machine quilting, because of the mechanics of moving the quilt in many directions. Using the same color thread in the bobbin as on the top will conceal most issues as long as the tension is properly adjusted.

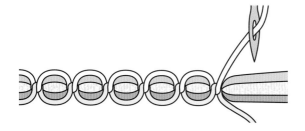

Motifs stitched with poor tension

Motifs stitched with improved tension

Motifs stitched with perfect tension

FINDING THE BEST TENSION

For most sewing machines, the stitch will look better when the top tension is lowered. Adjust the top tension first, adjusting the bobbin tension only if necessary. If it's impossible to balance the tension completely, it's better to have top threads pulled slightly to the back than to have bobbin threads showing on the top.

1 Prepare the machine for free-motion quilting as outlined in "The 12-Step Setup."

2 Using the same fabrics and batting that will be used in the quilt project, free-motion stitch a 3" line without changing the tension settings. Inspect the line.

3 Lower the tension one step or number and stitch another 3" line. Inspect the line. Does it look better or worse? If it looks better than the first line, lower the tension again and stitch another line.

4 Inspect this line of stitching. Does it look better or worse?

5 Continue lowering the tension and stitching lines until the newly stitched line looks worse than the previous one.

6 Tweak the tension between the final two lines to find the perfect sweet spot for your stitches.

Top tension too tight

Top tension still too tight

Better top tension

Good top tension

Good top tension with poor bobbin tension

Bobbin tension too tight (back of quilt shown)

Even Stitch Length

The quilting stitches, within a line and throughout the quilt, should be relatively even. The length of the stitch is determined by how fast you move the quilt relative to the speed of the machine. The perfect stitch length is a matter of preference and may differ depending on the size and style of the project. Creating even stitches is one of the most challenging aspects of machine quilting, so be patient!

EXERCISE: CREATING EVEN STITCHES

Creating even stitches is a matter of finding your personal quilting rhythm, which takes a great deal of time and patience. This quilting exercise can help you find a speed that works best for you and can be used as a warm-up exercise as well.

1 Set up your sewing machine for quilting.

2 Create a small quilt sandwich (fat-quarter size or smaller).

3 Choose an easy quilting motif or simple wavy lines.

4 Stitch the motif at your normal speed for two minutes.

5 Stitch at a much slower speed for two minutes.

6 Stitch at a much faster speed for two minutes.

7 Stitch at any comfortable speed for two minutes.

Whenever you're quilting a project, be aware of your quilting speed. Many quilters stitch better when they force themselves to quilt a little faster than their natural speed, as this forces greater concentration. However, some speed demons can definitely benefit from slowing down!

Varied Length

While most of your quilting stitches should be even, some shapes require shorter stitches. The stitches on small circles, spirals, and flower petals will be shorter than the stitches on larger or less-detailed motifs like Deirdre's Diamonds (page 130). It's not necessary for all the stitches in different motifs to be the same size.

Make a Sample!

To ensure the perfect stitch, recheck your stitches before beginning any project, at the start of stitching each day, and whenever changing the thread, bobbin, or needle.

Use shorter stitches when creating offset rows of spirals.

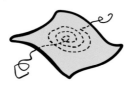

Refining Stitching Technique

In addition to creating "The Perfect Stitch" (page 20), several other techniques will improve the overall look of your quilting. Choosing well-designed motifs, understanding stopping points, and knotting off judiciously can make a world of difference when it comes to refining your machine quilting.

Avoiding Stitch Buildup in Open Motifs

Whenever a buildup of stitches is created by overstitching or by converging stitching lines, a focal point will be created within the quilting design. This can be a desired result. For example, in the Spiderweb motif (below and on page 94), some of the web lines are overstitched to make them more prominent.

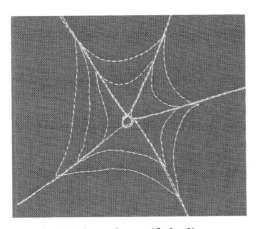

In the Spiderweb motif, the lines are overstitched to give them more definition.

Several converging lines in a pattern can create an undesired focal point. To avoid this, simply modify the design slightly. Instead of allowing the stitching lines to converge or overlap in a closed shape (creating a buildup of stitches), it's often better to leave a small gap between two lines—leaving the motif "open." You'll prevent the undesired focal point and the motif will still read as a closed shape.

Where a closed motif begins and ends, as at the side of the spool in Spools of Thread (page 119), there's a potential for thread to build up and create an unwanted focal point.

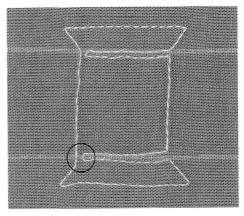

To avoid an undesirable focal point, leave a small gap between the starting and ending stitches. The pattern will look as though it's closed, but there won't be a distracting buildup of stitches.

All of the motifs in this book are designed either to avoid converging lines or to use them to create planned focal points. Use careful stitching technique to create the desired effect.

When the leaf of Holly and Berries (page 46) is stitched so that lines overlap, undesirable focal points emerge at the base of each leaf.

When stitched properly, the holly leaf has a small gap between the right and left sides of each leaf, allowing space for the stitching line to exit without crossing any other stitches.

Stopping Points

When machine quilting, you'll need to stop frequently to adjust either your hands or the quilt. Knowing where to stop within each motif will help you keep the stitching line smooth. With each stop and start, there's a greater chance of creating uneven stitches. To camouflage this effect, avoid stopping in the middle of a smooth line. Instead, stop wherever there's a change of direction.

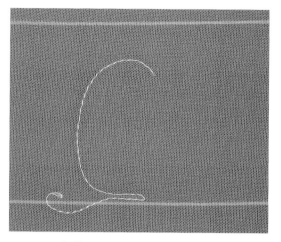

For smooth lines, stitch a complete curve and then stop where the lobes of the pumpkin meet.

When stitching the Perfect Pumpkin (page 102), avoid stopping mid-curve.

Crossovers

Crossovers occur any time one stitching line is stitched over a previous line. Patterns like Silly Spirals (page 126) include crossovers and look lovely. Other motifs, like the Classic Marigold (below and on page 80), are designed to avoid crossovers. In that motif, the stem is stitched first and the petals are stitched clockwise and counterclockwise to avoid crossing over the stem line. Choose well-designed motifs or modify your technique to create the best look for your quilt.

The Classic Marigold motif was designed to avoid crossovers.

Notice how different the flower looks when the stem crosses the petals.

Tracing or Overstitching

Tracing and *overstitching* are two terms used to describe stitching on top of a previously stitched line. Overstitching is often used to travel within a motif or from one motif to another. When done in lightweight thread, overstitching may have no visual impact. When stitched with heavier or decorative thread, however, the double or triple line can be distracting. Often you can modify a motif during the design phase to avoid tracing. Sometimes the only way to avoid tracing is by knotting off. Stitch samples, and judge the design carefully, to determine the best combination of overstitching and knotting off.

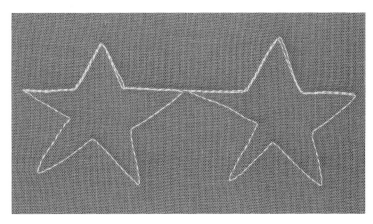

Traveling within Stars and Spirals (page 70) via overstitching leads to an unwanted focal point on top of the star.

Stitch above the top of the star to prevent the unwanted focal point—and to add some extra dimension to the design.

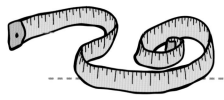

Knots

Several types of knots are used by machine quilters. Choose the knot that best suits the motif, the quilt, your time constraints, and the thread. All of the following knots, when made correctly, will hold up well to normal quilt use.

Tied and Buried

A hand-tied knot is the least noticeable but the most time-consuming to create. For this knot, both the beginning and ending thread tails are tied after the stitching line is complete. To make a tied-and-buried knot, pull the bobbin thread to the top of the quilt and tie it with the top thread into a double knot. Thread both tails into a hand-stitching needle and insert the tip of the needle into the edge of the nearest stitch. Pull the needle and threads between the quilt layers, tug until you hear the knot pop into the batting layer, and then pull the needle back up to the surface of the quilt and clip the thread tails.

Use a hand-sewing needle to bury the knot in the batting.

Stitch in Place

While a stitch-in-place knot is slightly more noticeable than the tied-and-buried knot, it's much quicker. To make it, pull the bobbin thread to the top and hold it and the top thread tautly as stitching begins. Stitch several very small stitches in place, and then begin stitching the motif. Trim the tails as soon as it's convenient to stop stitching. End the stitching line in the same way, making several small stitches in place, and trim immediately.

Many computerized sewing machines have programmable knots for quilting that are variations of the stitch-in-place knot.

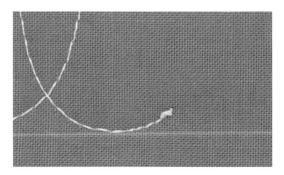

Sew several small stitches in place to begin and end a stitching line.

Curlicue Knot

The curlicue knot is fast and designed to be noticeable. This knot takes advantage of the focal point created any time there is a buildup of thread, and the knot becomes an attractive part of the stitching design. Form the knot by making very small stitches and then overstitching them to secure. As for the stitch-in-place knot (page 26), pull the bobbin thread to the top and hold it with the top thread to begin stitching. Using very small stitches, sew a small curl in the opposite direction of the stitching line. Reverse directions, stitching over the curl, and then begin stitching the planned motif. Trim the threads as sewing continues. To end a line of stitching with a curlicue knot, simply add an overstitched curl and trim.

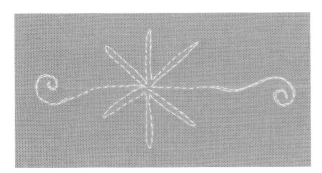

Curlicue knot at the end of a stitched line

Trimming the Bobbin Thread

When using the stitch-in-place (page 26) or curlicue knot (page 26) at the end of a stitching line, it's easy to trim the top thread, but the bobbin thread remains underneath the quilt. To bring up the bobbin tail for trimming, follow these easy steps.

1 Raise the needle and the presser foot to release the thread in the tension discs.

2 Push the entire quilt away from you 6" to 8" to create slack in the threads.

3 Pull the quilt back under the needle to create a loop of bobbin thread.

4 Lower the presser foot and drop the needle in or near the last stitch.

5 Raise the needle and the presser foot and tug the threads so the bobbin thread is accessible. Trim all of the threads and begin a new line of stitching.

Surgeon's Knot

A variation of the tied-and-buried knot (page 26), the surgeon's knot is used whenever one of the thread tails is very short. This usually occurs when a thread breaks or the bobbin runs out unexpectedly. Begin by carefully unstitching the pattern back to an inconspicuous place within the motif, far enough back to have one of the tails be at least 3" long. Pull the bobbin thread to the top. Hold a pair of tweezers in one hand and wrap the longest thread tail around the tip of the tweezers. Open the tweezers and pull the shorter thread tail through the loop created around the tweezers. Repeat to tie a double knot. Thread the tails into a hand-sewing needle and bury the knot as described on page 26.

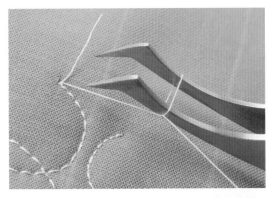

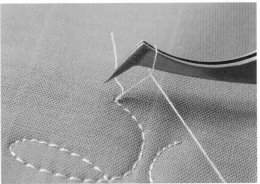

Make a surgeon's knot when a thread breaks or the bobbin runs out unexpectedly.

Design Considerations

The primary function of machine quilting is to join the three quilt layers. This task can be accomplished with basic allover quilting or tying. With a little planning, however, the quilted line can be more than functional; it can also enhance the overall beauty of even the simplest quilts.

Ideally, a broad outline of the quilting should be determined during the quilt-planning stage and while choosing fabrics. Use 28-, 30-, or 40-weight thread on prints for more visual impact. To highlight a quilting motif, choose solid or nearly solid fabric. Use good design principles to create balance, variety, contrast, and unity within the quilt, and doodle or stitch samples to determine the best scale for each motif used in the quilting design.

Balance Quilt Density

Balance the density of the quilting throughout the quilt to keep the design cohesive and prevent distortion in the quilt. Some areas can be more densely quilted than others as long as those areas are distributed evenly across the quilt. Areas that are heavily quilted tend to recede and areas that have less stitching tend to move forward or "pop." Balancing heavily quilted areas with lightly quilted areas is often used to create focal points within a quilt. For example, dense quilting around an appliqué will make the appliqué more noticeable.

Repeat and Vary

One of the easiest ways to design the quilting for a quilt is to choose just a few motifs and repeat them throughout. Repeating elements create balance and unity. To add interest, stitch variations of the same motifs in squares, triangles, rectangles, and borders.

To keep things simple, repeat a motif, such as the Perfect Poinsettia (page 38), in square blocks throughout the quilt.

Vary a pattern by adding partial motifs in triangles.

Add interest to your quilting by stitching slight variations of a motif. The Windowsill Garden (page 78) motif is more interesting when the design is repeated with small variations to the flower or the flowerpot.

Strive for a Hand-Drawn Look

As you stitch, remember that we're striving for a hand-drawn look, not pantograph or ruler perfection. Imperfections in the stitching line give the quilting personality and add interest to the quilt. Have fun when you're quilting and don't be afraid to make mistakes. Don't tear out any quilting lines until the entire quilt is finished (unless the mistake is poor tension). After the entire quilt is complete, judge the quilting in its entirety and then decide if any areas require restitching.

Contrast

Contrast simply means difference. Our eye quickly notices difference. Use contrast to draw attention to and highlight quilted elements. Contrast shape, thread, and density to create visual interest within the quilting line.

SHAPE CONTRAST

Combine curvy and linear motifs to create contrast between shapes. For example, in the bottom photo below, the simple straight lines stitched around Easy Breezy Flower (page 72) create a dynamic combination, whereas the spirals (page 18) stitched around the same flower motif have less impact. Whenever possible, stitch curvy motifs adjacent to linear or geometric motifs for the greatest appeal.

When the Easy Breezy Flower is combined with straight-line quilting, shape contrast is greatly improved.

Combine curvy and geometric motifs for visual impact. Pairing similar shapes, like Easy Breezy Flower and spirals, creates minimal shape contrast.

THREAD CONTRAST

Use thread color to either create or minimize contrast. Match the thread color to the fabric to create subtle texture. Choose a high-contrast thread if you want the quilting to stand out.

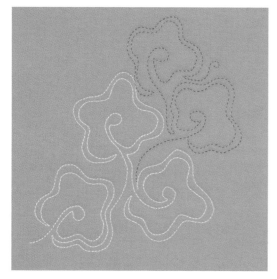

The Easy Breezy Flower motif stitched in blue creates subtle background texture, but it becomes the focal point when stitched in contrasting white thread.

Because the thread closely matches the fabric, the Windowsill Garden motifs are barely visible.

DENSITY CONTRAST

The density of the quilting can also create contrast. Stitch motifs that are widely spaced (such as the Jack-o-Lantern on page 86) next to motifs that are closely spaced (such as Moon and Stars on page 129). While both motifs remain distinct and visible, the more open motif will be seen first.

Create contrast by combining open motifs with closely spaced motifs.

Scale and Variations

You can vary the size or scale of a motif based on the size of the block or quilt. It's very important to test the scale of any motif by doodling (page 16) the quilt design.

Some motifs, like Jack-o-Lanterns, can easily be resized to fit any block or border.

ENLARGING A MOTIF

There are a variety of ways to enlarge any quilt motif, as you'll see here and on the following page. However, be mindful that it can be difficult to maneuver a large quilt to complete a motif that is greater than 10" to 12".

Replicate at a larger scale. The easiest way to enlarge a motif is to simply stitch it at a larger size. As the size increases, however, a motif can sometimes look too sparse. Stitch a sample to test the size of the motif before adding it to a quilt.

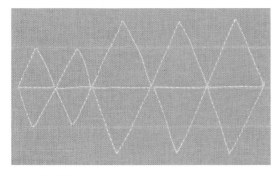

Motifs like Deirdre's Diamonds (page 130) can be enlarged to fit any space.

Not So Stiff

It's a misconception that dense quilting creates stiff quilts. Stiffness is a function of batting. While a newly quilted quilt may seem tight at first, with use it will become as soft as any quilt with minimal stitching.

Add rows. Many motifs can be enlarged by adding more rows or rounds. For example, flower motifs like the Classic Marigold (page 80) can easily be enlarged this way.

Increase the scale of a motif by adding more rows or rounds of the design, as with the extra row of petals shown here.

Echo stitch. Echo stitching is a great way to enlarge a motif while maintaining its visual impact. An enlarged motif often benefits from a single or double row of echo stitching.

Make a mirror image. Mirror imaging is an excellent way to enlarge a border motif. Motifs like Three Lucky Clovers (page 54) create beautiful, complex borders when expanded this way.

Increase the motif size by echo stitching around each part of the design.

Stitch a mirror image of a border motif and a whole new design emerges!

Exploring Corner Options

Many border motifs are too complex to stitch in a continuous line around the corner. Use the corner squares as a design opportunity. Try one of these creative corner methods or design your own.

One way to turn the corner with a border motif is to stitch to the end of the row and knot off before beginning the perpendicular border.

Another corner option is to add a different motif in the corner.

A corner is a great place to add your initials and the date.

Tips for Quilting "The Big Quilt"

Your quilt top is complete and it's a masterpiece! You've decided to quilt it yourself—congratulations! Whether you are stitching on a machine with a 7" harp space or on a long-arm quilting machine, be confident! With perseverance, you *can* quilt a king-size quilt on any machine.

Be patient and allow yourself sufficient time to enjoy the process. Machine quilting is faster than hand quilting, but it's not fast! Allow yourself ample time to doodle, create thread and batting samples, and experiment with new motifs.

Doodle first! As soon as you start piecing the quilt, begin doodling quilting motifs. Audition the motifs in the shapes and sizes from your quilt.

Plan the quilting design. Choose a few motifs to begin designing the quilting. Use your old favorites, and be sure to try a few new motifs with each quilt. Pick at least one curvy and one linear or geometric motif for good contrast. You don't need to design the entire quilt before you start quilting.

Prints conceal and solids reveal machine quilting. Design your quilt accordingly. Save elaborate quilting designs for solid or nearly solid areas of your quilt, and add simple quilting or stitch in the ditch for more patterned areas.

Prepare your fabrics well. Press and starch the backing fabric. The starch helps the quilt glide on the surface of the sewing machine. Press the quilt top. Wrinkles are very difficult to remove after machine quilting.

Baste the quilt sandwich very well. Whether using pins or spray basting, begin by securing the bottom layer to a surface before layering the batting and quilt top. Check the back of the quilt for wrinkles or bunching before proceeding to the quilting phase.

Support the quilt. Do not fight gravity. Add tables or an ironing board all around the quilt surface to prevent the quilt from dragging. If possible, position the sewing table against a wall or corner to keep the quilt from falling off the table.

Stabilize the quilt. Stabilize the long horizontal and vertical axes of the quilt by stitching at 6" to 10" intervals. If possible, follow the lines of a block and stitch in the ditch with a walking foot or stitch a wavy line with a free-motion quilting foot. Once the quilt is stabilized, you can quilt in any area of the quilt without the risk of distorting the layers.

Get to know your quilt. Stabilizing the quilt may take several hours. Use this time to plan the next steps of the quilting process. Plan which areas will benefit from stitching in the ditch, simple quilting, and more elaborate quilting motifs.

Get a Grip. Use gloves, Grip and Stitch discs, hoops, or small squares of waffle foam (for throw rugs) to grip your quilt while stitching. Try the pinch method—pinch a small amount of the quilt sandwich between the thumb and forefinger of your left hand to help maneuver the large quilt as you stitch.

Use your elbow. Use your left elbow and forearm to help guide the quilt and prevent it from dragging or pulling on the area under the needle.

Clear one small area at a time! You only need to clear one small space at a time for quilting. Scrunch the quilt in any way necessary to smooth out a 5" to 6" area for quilting. Stop with the needle down and do it again. Step by step, fill small areas of the quilt and soon the entire quilt will be complete!

Small motifs on big quilts. One of the hardest things to free-motion quilt on a large quilt is a long, swooping line. It's difficult to maneuver a large quilt quickly and smoothly for more than a few inches at a time. Instead, choose smaller motifs to minimize the working area of each pattern.

Keep it simple! Stitch simple motifs in heavily patterned areas or where the block has a lot of piecing. Consider stitching in the ditch or using outline quilting to emphasize the shape of the block. Quilt more complex motifs where the motif will be more visible.

Take frequent breaks. Stitch for short periods of time and then give yourself a break. This will help both mentally and physically. Step back and look at your work. Enjoy small accomplishments while giving your neck and wrists a break from the prolonged posture.

Flag mistakes. If you make mistakes while quilting, mark each one with a flagged safety pin. Once the quilt is completely finished, go back and decide—in the grand scheme of the quilt—whether the errant stitches require reworking. The flag will help you distinguish the safety pin from a basting pin.

To make a flagged safety pin,
add a piece of ribbon to any safety pin.

Enjoy the process! Stitch motifs you enjoy with thread you love. Entertain yourself by stitching random motifs like owls, birds, dog bones, and hidden messages within your quilting line. Stitch jokes, prayers, or poems into the quilt and wait to see if your friends and family notice…maybe future generations will!

Troubleshooting Tips

You can avoid most technical problems by carefully walking through "The 12-Step Setup" (page 7) before starting to free-motion quilt. By keeping your machine well-oiled and cleaned, and by using a single-hole throat plate and the correct needle size, you can stitch right past the most common issues of skipped stitches, tension troubles, and thread breakage.

Quick Fixes

When problems do arise, try the following Quick Fixes first.

✖ **Tension problems or thread loops.** Clean and oil your machine, rethread top and bobbin.

✖ **Broken thread.** Replace the needle, change needle type or size, rethread top and bobbin.

✖ **Skipped stitches.** Clean and oil your machine, change needle size or type, rethread top and bobbin.

Thorough Check

If the quick fixes don't solve the problem, run through this more comprehensive list. If you continue to have sewing errors, consult a sewing machine technician.

1. THREAD AND THREAD PATH

✖ Is the thread path—from spool to machine—clear?

✖ Is thread getting caught on something, such as the edge of the spool?

✖ Are you using good-quality thread?

✖ Is the thread old or damaged?

✖ Are all the thread guides properly threaded?

✖ Did you thread the machine with the presser foot in the "up" position to open the tension discs?

✖ Would using a cone holder and allowing the thread more time to unwind help?

2. BOBBIN

✖ Is the bobbin wound correctly? (Thread should be stacked and even.)

✖ Is the bobbin inserted correctly?

✖ Is the bobbin turning in the correct direction?

✖ Are you using the correct bobbin for your machine?

✖ Is there any tail of thread hanging off the bobbin that should be trimmed?

✖ Is there damage to the bobbin? (Even invisible damage may cause stitching errors.)

✖ Is there any thread or lint caught in the bobbin or bobbin case?

3. NEEDLE

✖ Is the needle damaged or old? (Even brand-new needles may have burrs.)

✖ Is the needle the right type of needle?

✖ Is the needle the right size for the thread you are using?

✖ Is the needle inserted correctly?

4. SEWING MACHINE

✖ Is the machine well-oiled and cleaned?

✖ Is there any damage or burrs on the throat plate or hook?

✖ Is there any lint or thread caught in the thread guides, tension discs, or bobbin?

✖ Did you lower the presser foot before stitching?

✖ Is the presser foot tension too high or too low?

✖ Do you have the latest software update on your sewing machine?

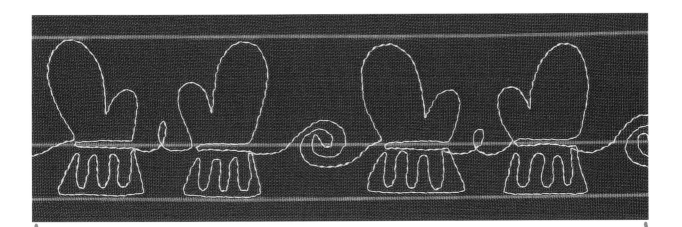

Winter

As winter approaches and the snow starts to fly, quilters are busy stitching holiday decorations and presents. Be sure to include a few sprigs of Mistletoe and Berries (page 44) as well as the ever-classic Perfect Poinsettia (page 38) on your quilts. Take time out to don your Woolly Mittens (page 40) and build Mr. Snowman (page 45)! If you're a beginner, start with the Pine Bough (page 50). More advanced quilters might like to combine all the motifs in a large wreath!

Perfect Poinsettia

The poinsettia is the essence of the Christmas season. This pretty flower can be stitched in a small square, or you can add several rows of petals to fill a large block. Each row of petals is tucked between the previous row, and then the swirls are added to give it a festive charm.

1 Stitch a cluster of small circles. Add a tapered petal.

2 Continue around the cluster, adding a total of five tapered petals.

3 To begin the next round of petals, echo stitch the last petal halfway up its side, then add a tapered petal between lower petals.

4 Echo stitch the next petal from the first layer, then add a second tapered petal. Continue around the flower, echo stitching the previous round and adding tapered petals.

5 When the petals are complete, echo stitch around the flower, adding swirls between each petal.

6 Stitch swirls in both directions for added interest.

Candy Cane Border

When stitched on red fabric or in a Christmas quilt, this motif adds a whimsical candy-stripe effect. Stitched on green fabric in a floral-themed quilt, this fabulous border looks more like a leaf.

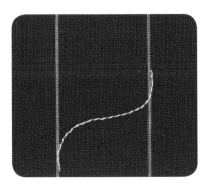

1 Draw two parallel guidelines. Sew several stitches on the left line and gently curve or *sweep* up toward the right line. Stitch on the right line a few stitches.

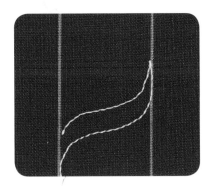

2 Taper downward a few stitches, then sweep to the left line, stopping just above the previous line of stitching.

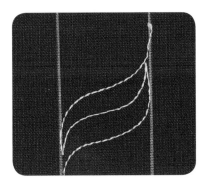

3 Sweep back to the marked right line, following the curve of your previous stitching. Stitch on the right line a few stitches.

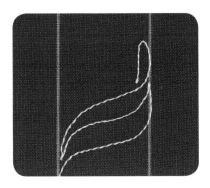

4 Curl downward to begin a wavy line from the marked right line to the left line.

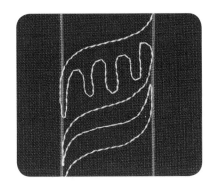

5 Continue stitching tight vertical waves, then sweep to the right line to begin the next motif in the border.

6 At the end of the row, add a spiral (page 18) or other decorative motif to create an interesting and easy corner treatment.

Woolly Mittens

Warm and woolly, these mittens add charm to any quilt border. Add a looping line between the motifs to change the border into a background fill, or stitch a pair of mittens into the corner square of a kitten quilt.

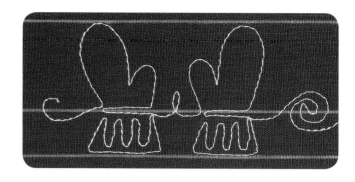

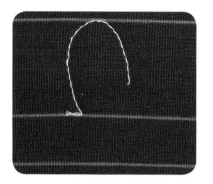

1 Draw three parallel guidelines. The upper space should be about twice as big as the lower space. Beginning on the centerline, stitch an upside-down *U* stopping above the centerline.

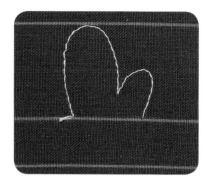

2 Add a smaller upside-down *U* ending on the centerline.

3 Stitch along the centerline to the starting point and closely echo stitch back to the thumb side of the mitten.

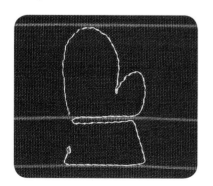

4 Stitch a small rectangle to create the cuff. Notice that I angled the sides of my cuff.

5 Add a wavy line or other decoration within the cuff, then add a short loop line to begin the right-hand mitten.

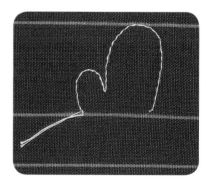

6 For the right mitten, stitch a small upside-down *U* first followed by a large upside-down *U*.

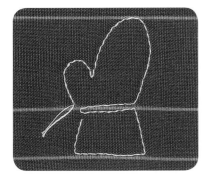

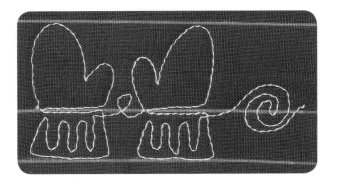

7 Stitch along the centerline to the left to the base of the thumb and back again. Add the cuff as for the left mitten.

8 Add the wavy line through the cuff, then stitch out of the pair of mittens and add a spiral "snowball" before adding the next motif in the border.

9 Create a single-row border by stitching multiple pairs of mittens.

Practice drawing designs here.

Snowballs and Snowflakes

Festive and whimsical, this combination of stars and spirals adds personality and fun to any quilt and looks great stitched horizontally as well as vertically.

1 Draw three parallel lines equidistant apart. Beginning on the centerline, stitch down several stitches. Add a stitched line, angling toward the left line. Closely echo stitch back to the center.

2 Stitch a short horizontal line to the left drawn line. Closely echo stitch back to the center.

3 Stitch down and to the left of the stitched centerline. Closely echo stitch back, past the center to the right drawn line.

4 Closely echo stitch back to the center.

5 Stitch a horizontal line to the right drawn line and echo stitch back to the center.

6 Stitch down and to the right side line. Echo stitch back to the center. Stitch a vertical line to begin the snowball.

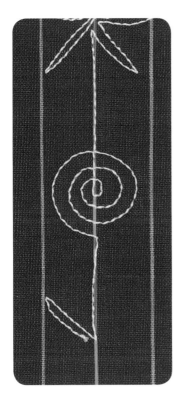 

7 Add a Loose Screws spiral motif (page 128), stitching counterclockwise to create a circle. Stop at the bottom edge of the spiral. Stitch a vertical line to begin the next snowflake in the pattern.

8 When stitched vertically, the offset stars and spirals create a festive tinsel effect on your quilt.

Practice drawing designs here.

Mistletoe and Berries

Mistletoe with its white berries is said to bring good luck to people who kiss beneath it. Add this motif to give a modern look to a quilt border, or cluster the leaves and berries to create a background fill.

1 Draw three parallel guidelines. Stitch a cluster of three round berries along the centerline. Stitch a few stitches upward on the centerline.

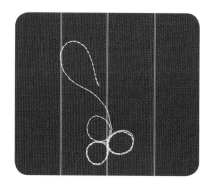

2 Sweep from the centerline to the left guideline and curl around toward the centerline to create a lobe-shaped leaf.

3 Sweep from the centerline to the right sideline, curling around to create another leaf.

4 Stitch upward along the centerline a few stitches and add a third leaf.

5 Add a circle to begin the next cluster of berries in the row.

Mr. Snowman

For those who live in the snowy North, winter would not be complete without a snowman! This adorable motif will brighten any quilt and there's no need for perfect circles!

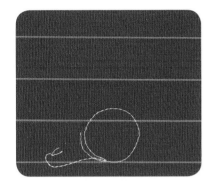

1 Draw four parallel guidelines. Stitch a curlicue knot on the bottom line. Stitch a clockwise circle, extending above the second line. Echo stitch the left side of the circle.

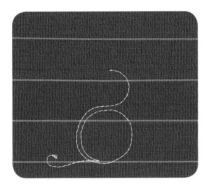

2 Stitch above the top of the first circle, then stitch a circle going counterclockwise.

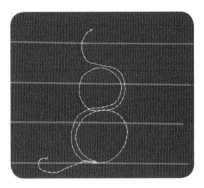

3 Echo stitch halfway around the second circle, then stitch the third circle going clockwise.

4 Echo stitch the left side of the head, stopping on top. Stitch a short horizontal brim, then a square top hat along the top line.

5 Complete the right side of the hat, and echo stitch the right side of Mr. Snowman's head. Add three loops to create a scarf.

6 Echo stitch the right side of Mr. Snowman and stitch along the bottom line to begin the next motif in the row.

Holly and Berries

Bright green and red all winter long, the holly plant is a winter favorite! It pairs well with berries and spirals, or Pine Boughs (page 50), and Mistletoe and Berries (page 44). Stitch the motif in a circle to create a wreath, in a row to create a border, or clustered to fill a background.

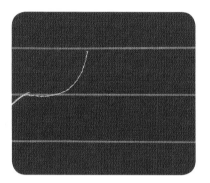

1 Draw three evenly spaced parallel guidelines. Beginning on the centerline, stitch a shallow scallop from the centerline to the upper drawn line.

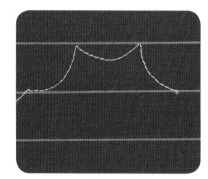

2 Stitch a shallow scallop along the upper line. Add a shallow scallop from the upper line back to the centerline.

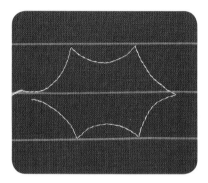

3 Complete the second half of the leaf by mirror-imaging the scallops on the first half of the leaf. Leave a small gap at the base of the leaf.

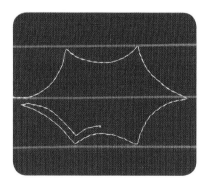

4 Echo stitch the *inside* of the holly leaf, again leaving a gap when you reach the starting point.

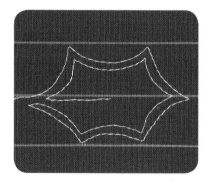

5 Stitch through the horizontal center of the leaf and exit through the leaf tip.

6 Add circle berries and spirals.

7 To use Holly and Berries as a background fill, echo stitch the center of the leaf, back to the base to begin the berry circles. Stitch a spiral or two and then begin the next leaf.

Practice drawing designs here.

Pretty Pinecone

A Pretty Pinecone is the perfect corner embellishment for any winter-themed border. Or stitch a cluster of pinecones in a wreath of Mistletoe and Berries (page 44) and Holly and Berries (page 46). When learning this motif, it's easiest if you start with a circle that's fairly small.

1 Draw a small circle the size you want your pinecone to be. At the top, stitch a short line and echo stitch back to the circle to create the stem.

2 Just below the stem, stitch a small semicircle and echo stitch back to form the top of the pinecone.

3 Stitch a row of scallops below the pinecone top, extending lower in the center to create the circle contour.

4 Echo stitch the scalloped line back to the right side and begin another row of scallops.

5 Add another echo-stitched row of scallops. On each row, extend the center scallops lower than those on the sides to develop the rounded contour of the pinecone.

6 Continue adding rows of scallops to fill in the drawn circle.

7 Add an echo-stitched scallop at the base of the pinecone.

8 Echo stitch around the entire pinecone, adding a holly leaf (page 46) or Pine Bough (page 50) embellishment near the stem.

9 Add two curls to the base of the pinecone to embellish it, and now it's a Pretty Pinecone!

Pine Bough

The Pine Bough is a simple motif that can be stitched in either a horizontal or vertical row, or clustered to fill other shapes. It's the perfect complement to motifs like Mistletoe and Berries or Holly and Berries (pages 44 and 46, respectively).

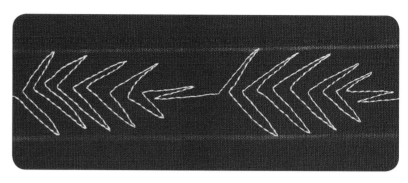

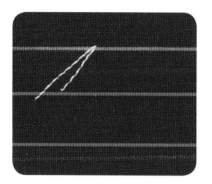

1 Draw three parallel guidelines. Beginning on the centerline, stitch at an angle to the top line and stitch back to the center, creating a narrow angle.

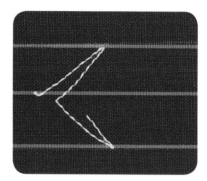

2 Stitch at an angle to the lower line and back toward the center.

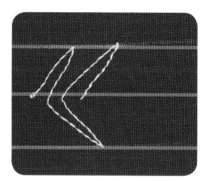

3 Continue stitching angled lines from the center to the sides and back to the center.

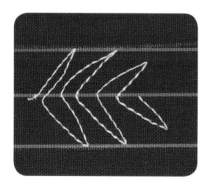

4 To taper the pine bough, stop the angled stitching lines short of the drawn lines before returning to the center at the tip of each motif.

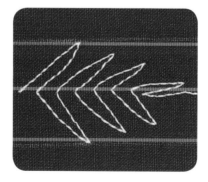

5 Stitch a horizontal "needle" to complete the motif. Stitch a horizontal line to travel to the next motif in the row.

6 To quilt a cluster, stitch back through the motif to the base to begin another bough or to add circles for berries.

Spring

As winter melts into spring, our thoughts turn to the garden. To fill a border, stitch one of the variations of Three Lucky Clovers (page 54) or a row of Daffodils (page 60). Occasionally tuck in Dancing Butterflies (page 53), Baby Bunny (page 58), or Baby Bird (page 68) to add a whimsical symbol of spring. If you're a beginner, start with the Lovely Carnation (page 56), which can be used as a border or background fill.

Silly Spiral Flower

Add a modern touch to any quilt with this simple little flower. Stitch it on a baby quilt, tea towel, or table runner for an extra bit of charm. Add a Baby Bunny (page 58) within the row for a whimsical look.

1 Draw two parallel guidelines. Stitch a curlicue knot on the bottom line, stitch to the right, then stitch a straight vertical line, stopping where you want the center of the flower to be.

2 Stitch a small spiral, crossing over the stem several times. End the spiral near the stem.

3 Add a smooth scalloped line around the center spiral.

4 Echo stitch the stem and add a pointed leaf halfway between the spiral and baseline.

5 Finish echo stitching to the baseline and stitch to the right to begin the next flower.

6 For a different look, echo stitch the stem to the baseline and stitch two narrow leaves.

Dancing Butterflies

Add a few Dancing Butterflies to your floral quilting motifs for a pretty surprise. They add a carefree element to children's quilts as well.

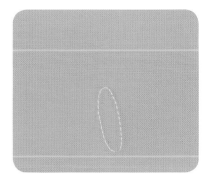

1 Stitch a narrow oval, clockwise, to form the butterfly body.

2 Echo stitch the left side of the oval. Add a small circle, stitching counterclockwise.

3 Echo stitch the right side of the circle. Add a short line with a curl. Overstitch the curl back to the circle.

4 Take one or two stitches to the left and add another overstitched curl. Echo stitch the left side of the small circle and begin the wings by stitching a sideways *U* shape.

5 Add a loop and a slightly smaller sideways *U* to complete the left wings. Closely echo stitch the bottom and right side of the oval, ending near the head to begin the right wings.

6 Add matching upper and lower wings on the right side. Add a loopy line to begin the next butterfly, or a curl to end a single motif for a corner block.

Three Lucky Clovers

To create more interesting quilting, stitch a motif multiple times but vary it. Here is not one, but three versions of clover! Aren't we lucky?

1a Draw three parallel guidelines. Beginning on the bottom line, stitch a shallow scallop to create the stem. Add a rounded petal, stitching clockwise.

1b Stitch a rounded vertical petal, leaving a small gap in the petal.

1c Add the right petal, and stitch a shallow scallop toward the bottom line.

1d If desired, echo stitch all three petals before stitching the final scallop.

2a Create the spiral clover by replacing the rounded petal with a spiral. Messy Spirals (page 18) also work great for this clover motif.

2b Add the top centered spiral petal.

$2c$ Stitch the third spiral on the right.

$2d$ Echo stitch the clover before continuing to the next motif.

$3a$ For the third clover option, stitch a rounded petal as in 1a, then reverse direction to add an interior rounded petal.

$3b$ Use careful stitching technique as you add the top and right petals to prevent a messy buildup of stitches in the center of the motif.

$3c$ Echo stitch the clover for a fuller look before moving on to the next clover.

Practice drawing designs here.

Lovely Carnation

Pink carnations are a symbol of a mother's love, while white carnations represent good luck. Every color of carnation is rich with symbolism. This beautiful motif looks great as a border and even better when stitched in staggered rows to fill a background.

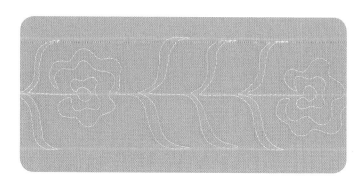

1 Draw three evenly spaced parallel guidelines. Stitch a curlicue knot below the centerline, then sweep from the centerline to the lower guideline.

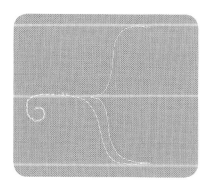

2 Echo stitch back to the centerline. Sweep up to the top guideline.

3 Echo stitch back to the centerline. Stitch along the centerline for several stitches, then sweep to the bottom line to begin another set of leaves.

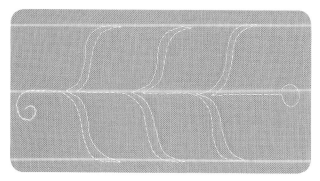

4 Stitch two or more pairs of leaves in the same way. Stitch along the centerline and add a small circle to begin the flower.

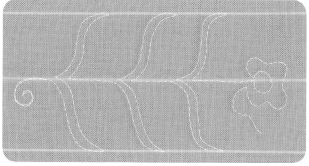

5 Stitch a wavy line around the center circle. Reverse direction at the stem to begin another round of wavy lines.

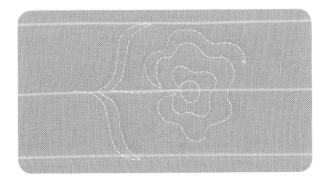

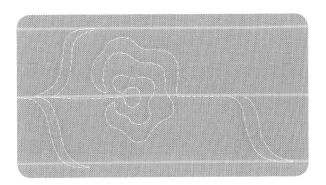

6 Stitch several rounds of wavy lines to fill the width of the border. End the last round on the centerline.

7 Stitch along the centerline to begin the next carnation in the row. The Lovely Carnation can be stitched horizontally or vertically to fill any border or background.

8 To create a background fill, stitch multiple rows, offsetting the leaves and flowers in each row.

Baby Bunny

Is there anything cuter than a baby bunny? This adorable motif looks sweet on an Easter quilt, a baby quilt, or any quilt for spring. Stitch one bunny peeking through a border of daffodils using the Daffodil motif (page 60) or a warren of bunnies to fill a border.

1 Draw three evenly spaced lines. Beginning at the bottom, stitch an oval, leaving a small gap.

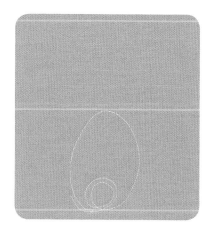

2 Stitch a circle inside the oval to create the tail; echo stitch the circle.

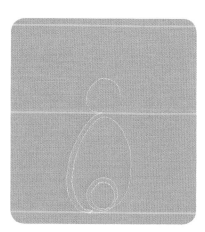

3 Echo stitch the left side of the oval. Add a small circle on top of the oval.

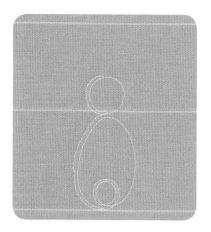

4 Echo stitch the left side of the small circle.

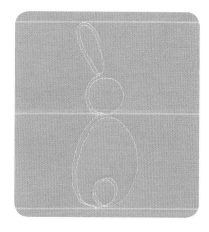

5 Add a loop angled up to the left to create an ear. Echo stitch the loop.

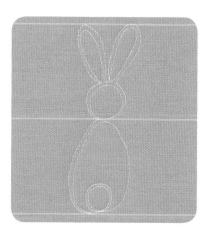

6 Add a loop angled up to the right. Echo stitch the loop and right side of the small circle.

7 Echo stitch the right side of the oval to the bottom. Stitch to the right, then curve up to the left to make the side of the basket. Make about six stitches to the right, then stitch straight up to form the handle.

8 Take two or three stitches to the right, then straight down to finish the handle. Make about six stitches to the right, then curve down to finish the basket. To add an optional pile of eggs, stitch to the right along the bottom line and make three small ovals.

9 To add flowers to a completed basket, closely echo stitch the basket from the bottom up to the base of the handle. Stitch out at an angle to make a stem, stopping halfway to make a pointed loop for a leaf. Stitch up to finish the stem, make a small circle, surround it with scallops, then stitch back down the stem to the base of the handle. Stitch a straight line right, crossing the basket handle, then make another flower and echo stitch around the basket down to the bottom line.

Practice drawing designs here.

Daffodil

Bright and cheerful, the daffodil is a happy harbinger of warm weather. A row of Daffodil designs will brighten any quilt border. Or combine the motif with the Easy Breezy Flower (page 72) to create a stunning background fill.

1a Draw three evenly spaced horizontal parallel guidelines. Beginning on the bottom line, stitch a straight stem, stopping slightly above the centerline. Add a small spiral.

1b Stitch a wavy line around the center spiral.

1c Add a kite-shaped petal near the stem.

1d   Continue adding petals around the center.

1e   Add five or six petals around the center and closely echo stitch the stem, stopping several stitches above the bottom line.

1f   Add a sweeping line to create the slender leaf. Echo stitch the line and add a narrow leaf on the right side.

1g   Add a bent leaf by echo stitching a bent line below one of the narrow leaves. Stitch to the bottom line and continue along to the next daffodil in the row.

2   To stitch a single motif, sweep out from the final leaf and make curlicues below the flower.

Iris

Symbolizing faith, wisdom, and hope, the iris is a perennial favorite of gardeners. Stitch this elegant motif in a border or set four flowers on point to fill a square block.

1 Draw three evenly spaced parallel guidelines. Beginning on the bottom line, stitch a vertical straight line and add a small oval above the centerline.

2 Add a lobed petal on the right side of the oval.

3 Repeat to add a mirror-image lobed petal on the left side of the oval.

4 Add a horizontal petal to the left side of the flower, above the centerline.

5 Stitch a horizontal petal to the right side of the flower, above the centerline.

6 Add two smaller downward-facing petals.

7 Closely echo stitch the stem back to the base of the flower. To create the leaf, stitch a straight line, angled upward to the left, ending with a circle that starts at the same height as the base of the original oval.

8 Add a tapered scallop to complete the left leaf.

9 Create the right leaf by stitching a straight line with a circle and adding a mirror-image tapered curve to complete the leaf. End a single Iris with a figure-eight loop at the base. Or stitch a wavy line to the right to begin the next flower.

10 When using the Iris motif in a border, handle corners by stitching on the diagonal and tapering the leaves to fit the space.

Hostas

Hostas are prized among shade gardeners for their wide variety of leaf sizes and shapes. Stitch a single row or several rows and create your own variety of hostas!

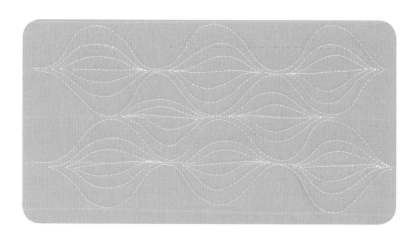

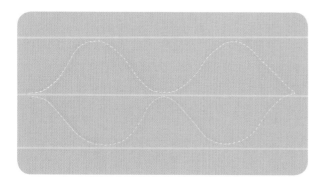

1 Draw three evenly spaced parallel guidelines. Beginning on the centerline, stitch a row of tapered scallops up to the top line. Reverse direction and add a row of mirror-image tapered scallops along the bottom.

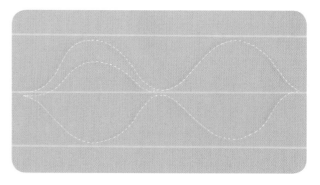

2 On the inside of the first leaf, echo stitch the upper tapered scallop. Avoid stitching over any previous line of stitching at the tip of the leaf.

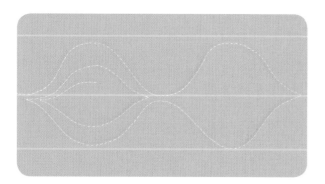

3 Echo stitch the lower tapered scallop and begin another row of echo stitching.

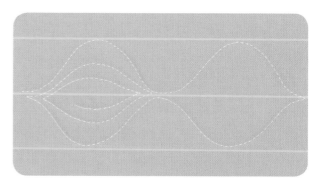

4 Complete the echo stitching on the top and bottom of the left leaf.

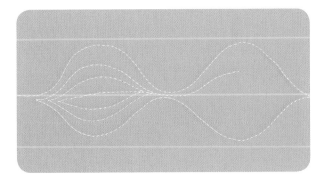

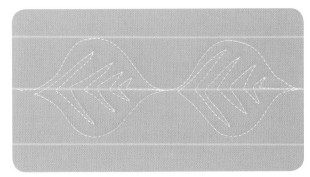

5 Stitch through the center of the leaf to begin filling the next motif in the row.

6 To add a little variety, fill each leaf with a Pine Bough (page 50).

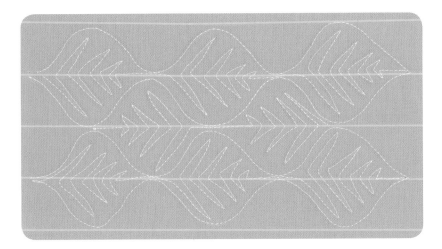

7 To fill a background with hosta leaves, begin by stitching several rows of tapered scallops (see Honeycomb on page 134) and then fill them in, one row at a time.

Practice drawing designs here.

Swirling Kite

Kite flying is the essence of carefree summer days. Add this charming motif to a baby's or child's quilt for a happy, whimsical touch.

1 Draw two guidelines in a cross formation. Beginning at the base of the cross, stitch a straight line from the base to the left side and then to the top of the cross.

2 Stitch the mirror image from the top to the right side of the cross and back to the bottom to complete the kite shape.

3 Stitch along the marked vertical line to the crossbar. Stitch the right horizontal line and echo stitch back to the center.

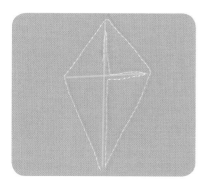

4 Stitch the top vertical line and echo stitch back to the center.

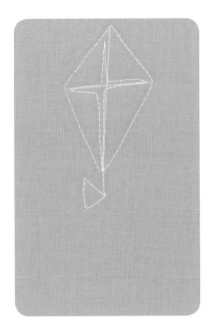

5 Stitch the left horizontal line. Echo stitch back to the center and down to the base of the kite. Stitch out of the kite to begin forming the tail and add a triangle on the left side of the tail.

6 Continue adding triangles or loops along a line to create the kite's tail. Add a loopy line to begin another motif.

7 Or, end with a curlicue knot (page 26) to complete a single motif.

8 To replicate kites on a windy day, angle kites this way and that for a design that's full of movement and fun.

Baby Bird

Baby Birds announce, "Spring is here!"
Stitch a single Baby Bird in the center of
a block or a flock of birds in a border.
Add quilted musical notes or little
messages around the Baby Bird for a
personal touch.

1 Stitch a half circle with the
curved edge along the
bottom. Stitch a horizontal line
back to the starting point.

2 Stitch a circle clockwise for
the head. Echo stitch back to
the top of the head. Add three
loops for a crest (head feathers).

3 To make an eye, curl into the
head, stitch a full circle and
overstitch back to the edge of
the head.

4 Add two small triangles to
form the beak.

5 Overstitch the bottom of the
head. Swoop into the body to
stitch a leaf-shaped wing. Closely
echo the bottom of the wing.

6 Add three loops for tail
feathers. If desired, stitch a
swirl below the bird, and continue
it to the next motif.

Summer

Whether you're designing a patriotic quilt or a quilt to commemorate a trip to the beach, this section is filled with a variety of borders, backgrounds, and fills. For a beach quilt, stitch Sand Dollars (page 76). For patriotic or nautically inspired quilts, stitch Stars and Stripes (page 74). If you're a beginner, start with the Easy Breezy Flower (page 72) and Classic Marigold (page 80). More advanced quilters will love the Windowsill Garden (page 78). Everyone should learn one of my favorites—Sunrise, Sunset (page 84)!

Stars and Spirals

Add a festive element to any quilt with Stars and Spirals. The density contrast provided by the echo stitching and spirals makes the stars pop in this edge-to-edge design.

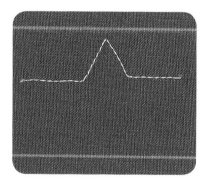

1a Draw two parallel guidelines. Beginning two-thirds of the way above the bottom guideline, stitch a short horizontal line, a triangle, and another horizontal line.

1b Stitch an inward triangle, down and toward the left, and then stitch back out toward the lower right, stopping just above the bottom guideline.

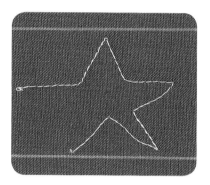

1c Stitch another triangle pointing upward.

1d Stitch another inward triangle to complete a star.

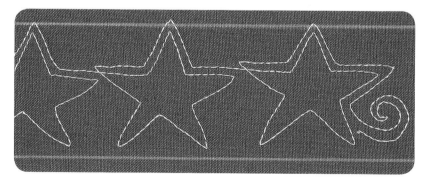

1e Echo stitch along the top of the star to begin another star in the row. Stitch stars to the end of the row, ending with a spiral.

1f Echo stitch along the bottom of each star in the row.

2a To fill a large area, add a spiral at the left end of the row, then tuck the tips of a second row of stars into the bases of the previous row.

2b Fill in any open areas between stars with spirals as you go.

3 For a single-row border of stars, add spirals as you echo stitch the top and bottom of the row.

Easy Breezy Flower

When you're looking for a way to quickly fill a background, this easy flower motif makes a pretty substitute for common meandering.

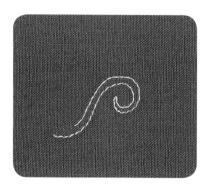

1 Stitch a curl and closely echo stitch it to make a stem.

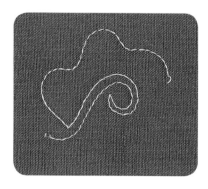

2 From the stem, add a bumpy line circling the curl.

3 Complete the bumpy line, ending close to the stem.

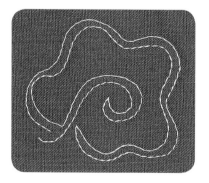

4 Reverse direction and echo stitch the flower, ending at the opposite side of the stem.

5 At the base of the flower, stitch another curl and echo stitch it to begin another flower.

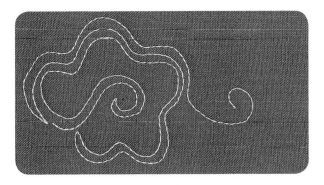

6 To start a new flower at a different location, echo stitch the flower and begin another flower at any point around the first flower.

7 To create a tightly clustered background pattern, tuck each of the petals into the adjacent flowers. Notice that the flowers don't all have the same number of petals. Stitch as many as you can to fill the area and then move on to the next flower.

Practice drawing designs here.

Stars and Stripes

Large and small stars combined with wavy lines create the essence of a flag and look patriotic on any quilt. Stitch this easy motif as a border or a background fill.

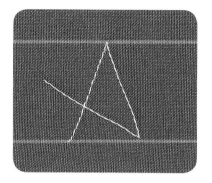

1 Draw two parallel guidelines. Beginning on the bottom line, add a simple star by stitching an open triangle and crossing at an angle to the left.

2 Stitch a horizontal line to the right.

3 Stitch down to the left to close the star shape.

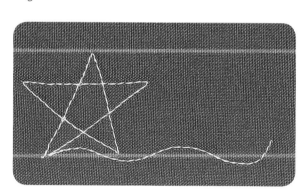

4 Stitch a wavy line below the star and to the right.

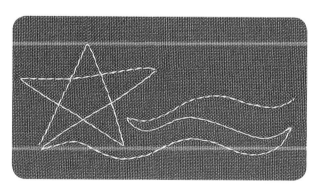

5 Stitch a wavy line back to the star and out again.

6 Stitch as many wavy lines as necessary to fill the space between the drawn lines, ending away from the star.

7 Add a small star extending above the top line.

8 Working downward, stitch several wavy lines to the right of the previous lines. End on the right side to begin the next large star and repeat the motif.

Sand Dollars

Sand Dollars provide a beautiful background fill for any quilt. Combine this little urchin with Starfish (page 82) to evoke warm, sunny days on the beach.

1 Stitch three short, radiating lines. You can overstitch for emphasis or closely echo stitch.

2 Stitch several stitches to the right, then up and around the three short lines.

3 Echo stitch the curved line.

4 Add three more spiky lines.

5 Curve up and around the three spiky lines.

6 Echo stitch the curve twice to travel to the top. Add spiky lines for the next sand dollar.

7 Curve up and over the spiky lines. You can echo stitch the curve two or three times, depending on where you want to travel.

8 Continue in the same way to create a tightly clustered background pattern.

Windowsill Garden

Stitch a single potted flower in the center of a quilt block or make several in a row to add charm to any quilt.

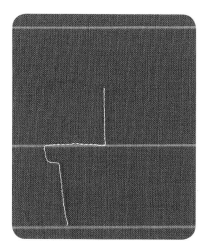

1 Draw three parallel guidelines. The upper space should be slightly larger than the lower space. Beginning on the bottom line, stitch upward at a slight angle. To make a rim on the pot, jog to the left, stitch up three or four stitches, and then stitch rightward on the centerline. Stitch a short vertical line upward.

2 Add a circle, spiral, or Silly Spiral (page 126) to create the center of the flower. End the shape at the base of the flower near the stem.

3 If you want to add petals to your flower, start stitching scallops around the center. Or omit the petals and go on to step 4.

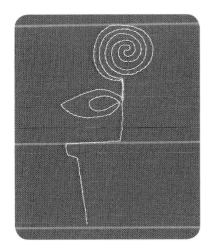  

4 Moving downward, closely echo stitch the stem for several stitches. On the left side, add a pointed leaf with a central loop.

5 Add a leaf on the right side, then closely echo stitch down the stem. Moving rightward, stitch a short horizontal line, then drop down three or four stitches. Jog in slightly to complete the rim.

6 Angle in slightly as you stitch down to the bottom line. Stitch to the left two or three stitches, and add a decorative element like rectangles or zigzags to fill the pot.

7 Stitch outward below the motif to begin the next motif in the row.

Practice drawing designs here.

Classic Marigold

The **Classic Marigold** is as easy to stitch as it is to grow. Tightly clustered rows of squared-off petals create its distinctive look. Stitch a few rows, or many, to fill a quilt block, or keep repeating motifs to replace stippling or meandering.

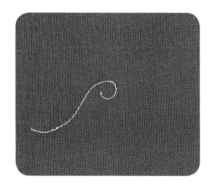

1a Stitch a curl to make a stem.

1b Reverse direction and tuck a squared petal right next to the stem.

1c Continue stitching counterclockwise, adding squared petals.

1d To begin a new row of petals, reverse direction at the stem, stitching a petal next to the stem and above the previous petal.

1e Continue adding petals clockwise. When you reach the stem, reverse direction to avoid overstitching it, then begin another row of petals.

1f To begin another marigold, stitch a stem curl outward from any point within the petals.

1g   Continue stitching marigolds as needed to fill your space.

2   To make a single Classic Marigold, add a row of echo stitching around the flower, then embellish with leaves and swirls.

Practice drawing designs here.

Starfish

The Starfish motif adds a whimsical, happy touch to any quilt. Stitch a single starfish in the center of a block, add a row of starfish to fill a border, or combine the motif with Sand Dollars (page 76) for a perfect summer background fill.

1 Draw a square. Stitch a spiral in the center, ending at the left. Then stitch up at a slight angle and back down to make a narrow vertical star point.

2 Stitch a narrow horizontal star point to the right of the spiral.

3 Add two more narrow star points that radiate toward the lower corners of the square.

4 Stitch a narrow star point to the left of the spiral, leaving a small gap between the first and final star points.

5 Stitch a counterclockwise curl and then echo stitch back.

6 Stitch another curl to fill the space between the two star points. Echo stitch the tip and down the side of the first point. Work around the star, adding curls between star points and echo stitching the tip of each point.

7 When you've reached the first set of curls, add a curlicue knot (page 26) to finish, or echo stitch along the top of the motif to begin another starfish.

Practice drawing designs here.

Sunrise, Sunset

Quickly fill a border of any size with this simple motif. If you're stitching a seamed border, use the seamlines as guidelines. Stitch wavy triangles for a shimmering variation.

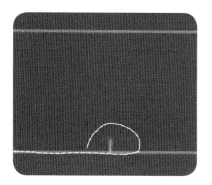

1 Draw two parallel guidelines. To keep even spacing between motifs, add chalk tick lines to mark the center of each motif. Beginning on the bottom line, stitch past the center mark. Add a scallop.

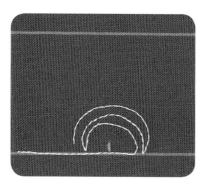

2 Echo stitch the scallop twice, ending on the left side of the motif.

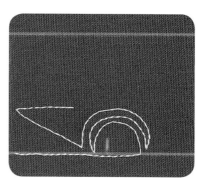

3 Add a triangle, ending a few stitches before the center scallop.

Mark Only When Needed

Draw vertical spacing lines in addition to the center markings only if necessary. Less marking means fewer lines to remove later!

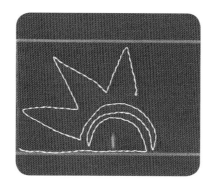

4 Add two more triangles around the scallop.

5 Continue adding triangles. For large borders, add more triangles if necessary. Then stitch along the baseline, past the next center tick mark, to begin the next motif. Stitch the motif as is or upside down for fun.

Fall

As summer fades and the kids go back to school, quilters everywhere return to their sewing studios and are inspired by the fall harvest. Stitch Perfect Pumpkin (page 102) or Sweetheart Apple (page 100) on any autumn quilt. Add the Jack-o-Lantern (page 86) or Spooky Spider (page 101) to a Halloween quilt. Be sure to try Braided Wheat (page 88)—a beautiful border motif that adds a new twist to modern or traditional quilts. If you're a beginner, start with the Japanese Lantern (page 90). It's quick and easy and doesn't require precise stitching.

Jack-o-Lantern

As Halloween approaches, it's time to bring out our Perfect Pumpkin (page 102) and turn it into a Jack-o-Lantern. Once you learn the basic face, be creative! Change the mouth to a circle and the eyes to diamonds or create your own combinations. Doodle first!

1 Draw two parallel guidelines. Stitch a curl at the bottom left, then curve up from the bottom line to stitch the letter *C*.

2 Add a short stem. If you're stitching a border row, vary the height of each pumpkin.

3 Stitch leftward under the stem a few stitches, then make a triangle for the left eye.

4 Stitch to the right two to three stitches and then add a second triangle.

5 Curve down, stitching a large backward *C* and leaving a small gap at the bottom of the pumpkin.

6 Curve up toward the left, then stitch a short horizontal line to the right, stopping between the triangle eyes.

7 Add a triangle nose and stitch a short horizontal line rightward.

8 Complete the right side of the mouth by curving down to the bottom line. Stitch along the bottom line to start the next Jack-o-Lantern.

9 Have fun with Jack, adding curly vines or spooky speech bubbles. He's the perfect addition to any Halloween quilt!

Braided Wheat

Braided Wheat is an elegant motif that looks great on both traditional and modern quilts. Use it in place of feathers in any border. It can be used horizontally or vertically.

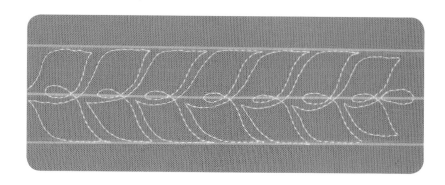

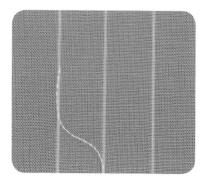

1 Draw three evenly spaced, parallel guidelines. Beginning on the centerline, sweep to the left line. Stitch along the left line for several stitches.

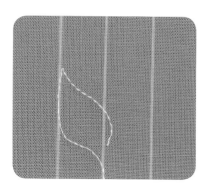

2 Curve back to the centerline.

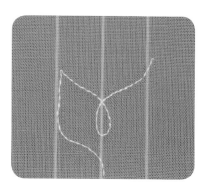

3 Stitch a small clockwise loop along the centerline and sweep up to the line at right.

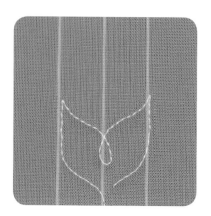

4 Stitch downward along the line at right and then sweep back to the centerline.

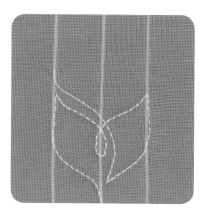

5 Stitch upward around the loop, sweeping over to the left line.

6 Stitch along the left line and curve back to the centerline. Add the loop.

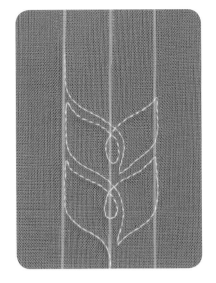

7 Repeat this pattern to continue the beautiful Braided Wheat motif.

8 To finish the motif, sweep upward to the centerline and stitch a loop.

Practice drawing designs here.

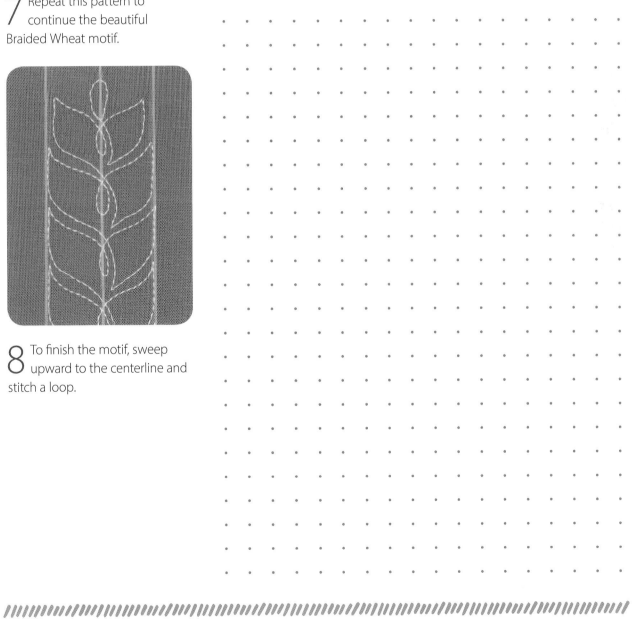

Japanese Lantern

The papery orange husks of the Japanese lantern plant surround perfectly round orange seeds. Add the quick and easy Japanese Lantern motif to your fall quilts. For a little more challenge, add round seeds between each lantern.

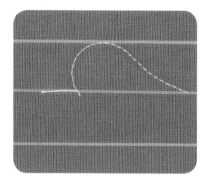

1a Draw three evenly spaced, parallel guidelines. Beginning on the centerline, stitch a half-heart shape by rounding to the upper line and then tapering back to the centerline.

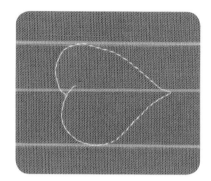

1b Stitch the mirror image on the lower half of the motif by tapering to the bottom line and then rounding back to the centerline.

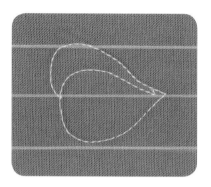

1c Stitch another half-heart shape, ending just before the previous line of stitching to avoid a buildup of stitches.

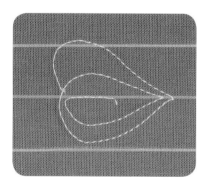

1d Stitch the mirror image on the lower half and then stitch on the centerline.

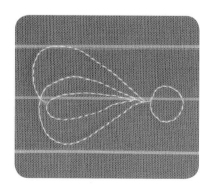

1e Stitch through the center of the motif to begin the next motif in the row. Add a circle or begin another lantern.

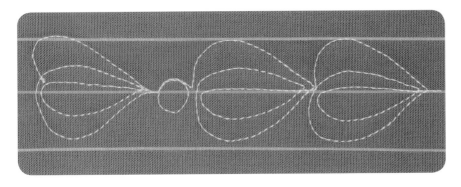

2a Add variety to the motif by randomly stitching round seeds.

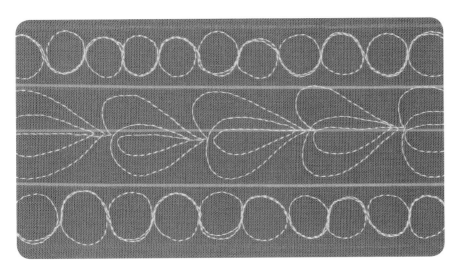

2b Alternate rows of Japanese Lanterns and round circles for a fuller border.

Practice drawing designs here.

Spooky Fence

The Spooky Fence is a great companion to Jack-o-Lantern (page 86) and the Perfect Pumpkin (page 102). The linear fence slats contrast with the rounded pumpkins for a perfectly spooky pairing.

1 Draw four parallel guidelines. Determine the best spacing of the lines for your quilt by doodling. Begin quilting on the baseline. Stitch a straight vertical line. Stop on one of the drawn lines and take two or three stitches to the left.

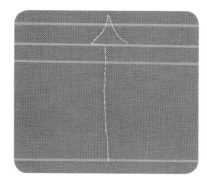

2 Stitch a small triangle.

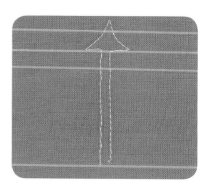

3 Stitch back down to the baseline.

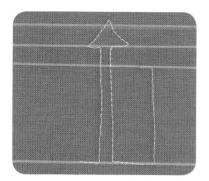

4 Stitch to the right, on the baseline. Stitch another, shorter slat in the fence.

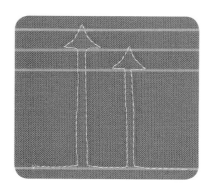

5 Stitch a small triangle and then stitch back down to the baseline.

6 Add a pumpkin (page 102) or other motif in the corner when stitching the Spooky Fence motif in a border.

Practice drawing designs here.

Spiderweb

Spiders and webs are often found on Victorian crazy quilts for good luck. Add this simple motif for luck or just for fun to your next quilt.

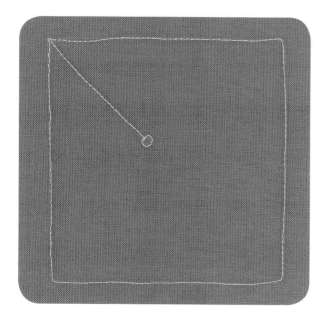

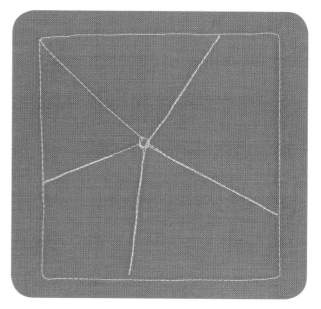

1 Stitch a square. Begin spinning the web in one corner of the block by stitching a straight diagonal line toward the center of the block and adding a small circle. The circle may be centered or off-center.

2 Add several overstitched lines from the center to the outer edges of the square. For the last overstitched line, stop a few stitches short of the center circle.

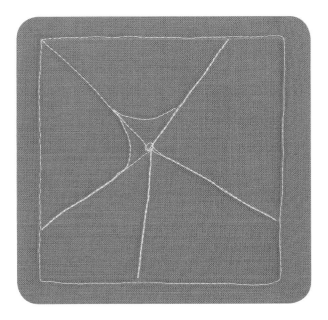

3 Add a scallop between the first two lines. Scallop to the next line.

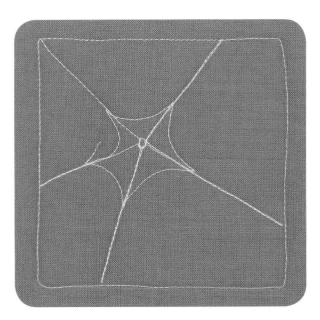

4 Continue working clockwise from line to line, adding scallops. Extend the last scallop in each row beyond the first row to begin another round.

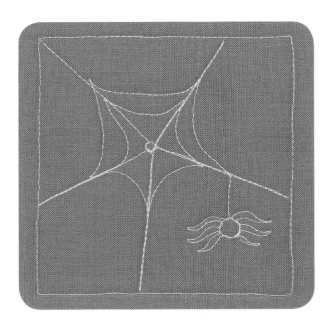

5 Stitch several rows of scallops and then add a dangling Spooky Spider (page 101).

6 The Spiderweb motif can easily be modified to fill a corner square.

Olivia the Owl

Add a whimsical touch to any quilt with this wise motif. Once you learn the basic outline, add your own embellishments to the head, wings, and body.

1 Draw four evenly spaced parallel guidelines. Beginning on the second line from the top, stitch a messy spiral (page 18), a small triangle beak, and another messy spiral, stopping next to the beak.

2 Beginning next to the beak, stitch a backward letter C.

3 Add an angular "cap" and a letter C to complete the owl's face.

4 Stitch an oval body.

5 Add a shallow scallop on the right side of the oval. Stitch a small rectangle for feet. Finish the basic shape with the left scallop wing.

6 Be creative embellishing Olivia the Owl. Here I used elongated scallops and Deirdre's Diamonds (page 130). In step 7 below, I used three rows of loops.

7 Echo stitch around the entire motif, adding three loops at the top of the head for feathers.

Practice drawing designs here.

Perfect Pear

Stitch a row of pears on a kitchen table runner or apron. Combine it with the Sweetheart Apple (page 100) and the Perfect Pumpkin (page 102) for a cornucopia of quilting!

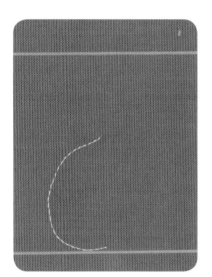

1 Draw two parallel guidelines. Beginning on the bottom line, stitch a letter C.

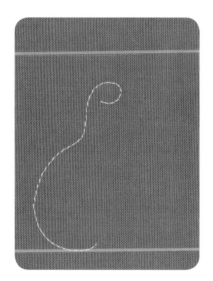

2 Stitch a short vertical line and curl around.

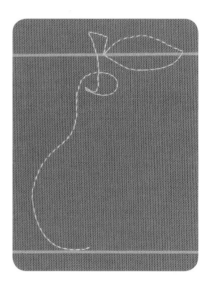

3 Take a few stitches back from left to right. Add a stem by stitching a short vertical line, then stitch over two to three stitches and back down. Stitch a leaf.

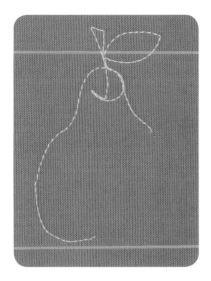

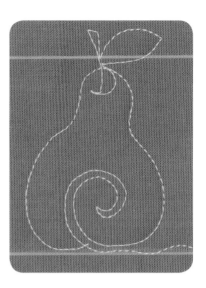

4 Begin stitching the right side of the pear by mirror-imaging the left side. Do not worry about perfect symmetry!

5 Complete the right side of the pear and then spiral into the center.

6 Echo stitch the spiral and stitch underneath the pear to begin the next motif.

7 To create movement within a border, vary the height of each pear and change the number and positioning of leaves.

Sweetheart Apple

Apples are the essence of autumn. Stitch a row of apples on a fall table runner or add them to a back-to-school gift for a teacher.

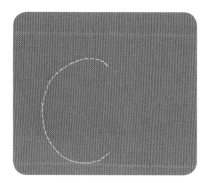

1 Draw two parallel guidelines. Beginning on the bottom line, stitch a letter *C*.

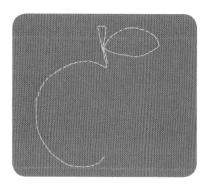

2 Add a short vertical line. To create the stem, stitch over two to three stitches and drop down a few stitches. Add a leaf.

3 Add a backward letter *C*.

4 Stitch a vertical line through the center of the apple. Overstitch or closely echo stitch back to the center and add four small loops. Overstitch the previous line back to the baseline to complete the motif.

5 For variety, after stitching the centerline in the apple, add a curl.

6 Echo stitch the curl and add an echo-stitched curl on the left side to create a heart shape.

Spooky Spider

While real spiders have eight legs, it's difficult to stitch all of them for this motif. Stitching only six legs still leaves you with an easily identifiable spider. If you're a purist, add more legs with careful stitching.

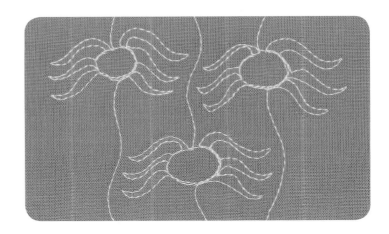

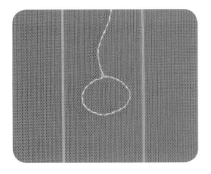

1 Draw two parallel guidelines. Stitch a wavy "silk" line, between the marked lines, to attach to the spider. Add a small oval.

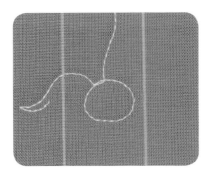

2 Beginning near the wavy line, stitch a curved leg to the left. Closely echo stitch the leg.

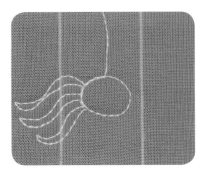

3 Add two more echo-stitched legs on the left side of the spider.

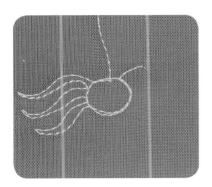

4 Stitch on the oval to the upper-right side of the oval.

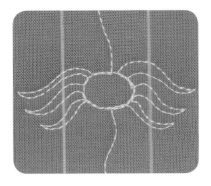

5 Add three echo-stitched legs on the right side of the oval. Stitch back along the oval to the bottom of the spider to begin the next "silk" line and the next spider.

6 Offset rows of six-legged spiders look really spooky!!

Perfect Pumpkin

This pumpkin is perfect because it looks good in every size. Combine small pumpkins, large ones, fat ones, and tall ones to create a spectacular fall border!

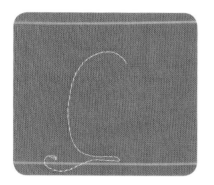

1 Draw two parallel guidelines. Stitch a curl at the bottom left, then curve up to stitch a letter C. (For border rows, vary the height of your pumpkins.)

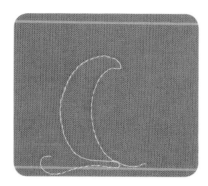

2 Stitch another shallow C downward from top to bottom.

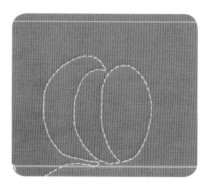

3 Stitch a clockwise oval, ending on the bottom guideline.

4 Stitch a backward letter C, stopping just above the oval.

5 Stitch leftward across the top of the pumpkin, then add a short stem.

6 Complete the stem and stitch a large backward C ending at the bottom. Continue stitching along the bottom line to begin the next pumpkin in the row.

Celebrations

Whether you're stitching a baby quilt, a wedding quilt, or a gift to commemorate an anniversary, there's a motif to help you celebrate. For a modern touch, add Hugs and Kisses (page 105) to a border or as a background fill. For a more traditional look, stitch Ribbons (page 104). Pretty Packages (page 110) and Cupcake (page 108) are fun for birthday quilts. If you're a beginner, start with Ribbons or String of Beads (page 112) and work your way up to Safety Pins (page 109). Whatever motif you choose, make every quilt a celebration!

Ribbons

Ribbons add a beautiful border to any quilt, from modern to traditional. Add circles or teardrops between the motifs to create different variations. This motif is quick and easy!

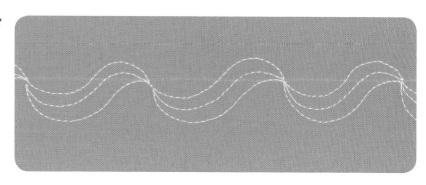

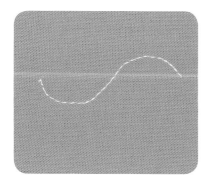

1 Draw a guideline. Stitch an S-shaped curve, starting below and ending above the guideline.

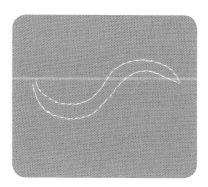

2 Echo stitch the curve.

3 Echo stitch back to complete the first wave of the ribbon.

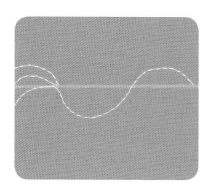

4 Add another S-shaped curve to begin the next wave.

5 Add circles or other embellishment between each wave.

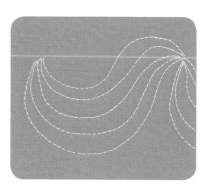

6 For a large border, add five or more echo-stitched lines.

Hugs and Kisses

Add a little love to a Valentine's Day quilt, baby quilt, or any gift quilt with this charming motif.

1 Draw two parallel guidelines. Beginning on the bottom line, stitch a wide angle, ending on the top guideline.

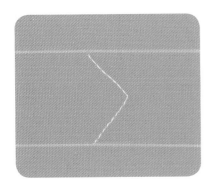

2 Closely echo stitch the upper line and stitch a letter *V*.

3 Add an inward angle.

4 Echo stitch the bottom with an upside-down *V*. Stitch under the *X* to the right to begin the next motif. Add a clockwise oval.

5 Reverse direction and echo stitch the *O*. Stitch under the *O* to begin the next motif, then add another *X*.

Baby Carriage

Welcome a new baby with this charming motif. Stitch the baby's name on the side of the carriage for a personal touch. This motif pairs well with Safety Pins (page 109).

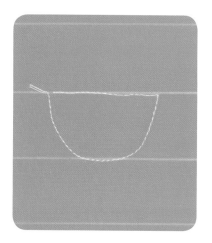

1 Draw four evenly spaced parallel guidelines. Beginning on the second line from the top, stitch a semicircle.

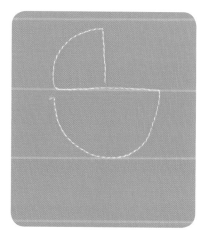

2 Add a curved line to the top guideline. Stitch a vertical line back to the semicircle.

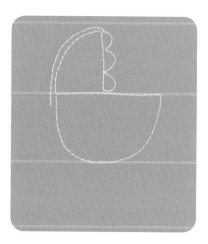

3 Add scallops along the vertical line, and then closely echo stitch the left side of the carriage.

4 Stitch under the carriage and add a clockwise spiral. Choose a messy, silly, or basic spiral (see page 18).

5 Stitch to the bottom of the carriage and a few stitches to the right. Add a counterclockwise spiral.

6 Echo stitch the front of the carriage and add a curled handle. Ready for a walk!

7 To add Baby's name to a carriage, echo stitch the curled handle and top of the semicircle, sweeping down at the left edge to begin stitching the name. End with a curlicue knot (page 26).

Cupcake

Turn your quilt into a celebration with this little confection. Or, add cupcakes to a birthday table runner. No one can resist a cupcake!

1 Draw three evenly spaced parallel guidelines. Beginning on the bottom line, stitch at an angle to the middle line. Add zigzags to the right. Stitch at an angle back to the bottom line.

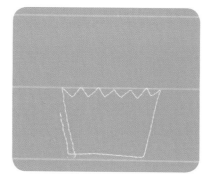

2 Stitch across the bottom guideline from right to left. Closely echo stitch the left side of the cupcake.

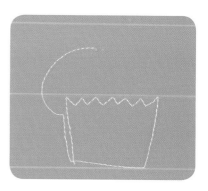

3 Add a shallow letter C.

4 Curve around, making a counterclockwise circle (or a heart or star). Continue the line around to the right side.

5 Add a deep zigzag or other embellishment.

6 Stitch under the motif to begin the next cupcake.

Safety Pins

While safety pins have given way to Velcro, this motif remains a lasting symbol of babyhood. Stitch the pins in a row to fill a border or add a loopy line between motifs to create an allover pattern.

1 Draw three parallel guidelines. The upper space should be smaller than the lower space. Stitch an upside-down *U*.

2 Stitch in two or three stitches and add a smaller upside-down *U*. Stitch from right to left back to the first stitch.

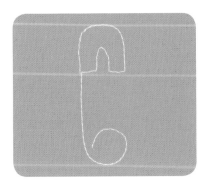

3 Stitch a vertical line and end with a circle.

4 Complete the circle, ending on the right side. Add a short straight line.

5 Overstitch the straight line and add a loopy line to begin the next motif.

6 Stitch the Safety Pins at different angles to create an interesting allover motif.

Pretty Packages

Stitch a row of Pretty Packages to complete a border or pair them with coal cars from the Circus Train as shown on the facing page. To fill a background, combine rows of packages.

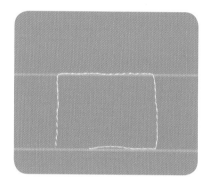

1 Draw two parallel guidelines. Beginning on the bottom line, stitch a rectangle leaving a small gap on the bottom near the start.

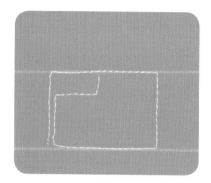

2 Closely echo stitch inside the left edge of the package, stopping about three-quarters up the side. Stitch a short horizontal line to the right, then stitch up to the top of the package.

3 Add three loops to form a bow.

4 Stitch down into the center of the package, then to the right side. Stitch down two to three stitches, then back toward the center.

5 Stitch to the bottom, over two to three stitches, and back up to the center.

6 Stitch to the left, stopping just before the side of the package. Echo stitch down the side then underneath the Pretty Package to begin the next rectangle.

7 Vary the height of the packages, stitching the tops on, above, or below the top guideline. Include tall and narrow packages and wide and narrow ones. Add ribbons after stitching the bows, if desired.

8 To finish a row of packages, sweep under the final package and end with a curlicue.

9 Closely stitch a row of packages along the top of coal cars from the Circus Train (page 122) to make a train bearing gifts.

String of Beads

Round beads are an easy border treatment for any quilt. Create your own variations by changing the shape from circles to teardrops or ovals. String a variety of bead shapes together for a festive holiday border.

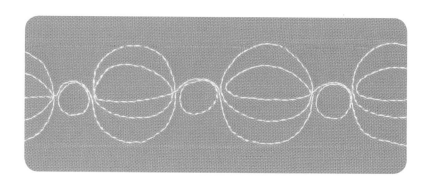

1 Draw two parallel guidelines. Begin stitching between the two lines. First stitch a counterclockwise circle, leaving a small gap.

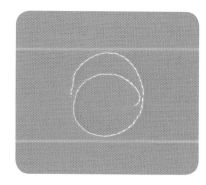

2 Add a scallop inside the circle, brushing the edge of the circle.

3 Add an upside-down scallop.

4 Stitch through the center of the circle.

5 Add a small circle to the right, stitching 1½ revolutions.

6 Begin the next bead on the string.

Just for Fun

Machine quilting is more fun when we add a bit of ourselves to the process. Add your quilting signature with notions like Sewing Scissors (page 114) or Tomato Pincushion (page 116). If you're a dog or cat fan—aren't we all?—add a Little Kitty (page 121) or throw your dog some free-motion-quilted Dog Bones (page 120). Because everyone loves the circus, try the Circus Train (page 122). More advanced quilters might want to fill the train cars with Spools of Thread (page 119) or Pretty Packages (page 110), or design their own circus animals to fill the cars!

Sewing Scissors

A pair of scissors seems complicated to stitch until you doodle its three simple parts: a long skinny triangle, a small square, and two circles. Add the shapes with light chalk lines to make stitching easier. This design works horizontally as well as vertically.

1 Draw three evenly spaced parallel guidelines. Starting on the middle line, stitch a narrow triangle.

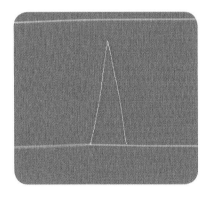

2 Stitch three to four stitches from right to left along the centerline. Add a vertical line, stopping just before the tip of the triangle. Closely echo stitch back down, then stitch to the left along the centerline.

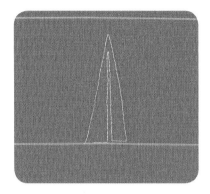

3 Stitch down several stitches and add a square underneath the triangle. Stop on the right side.

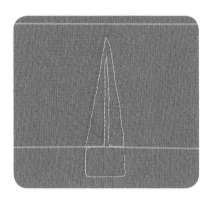

4 Add a small circle in the center of the square. If the scissors are large enough, add your initials or other embellishment in the square. End at the bottom of the square, stopping at the center.

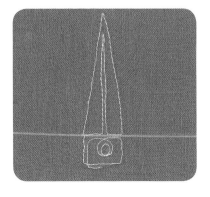

5 Next stitch a vertical line downward. Add a basic spiral or a messy spiral (see page 18). End next to the vertical line.

6 Stitch up to the center square, then back down again. Echo stitch the spiral.

7 Complete the echo stitching of the first spiral just under the square. Stitch down and add a counterclockwise spiral to begin the right handle of the scissors.

8 Complete the right-sided spiral, ending on the top of the spiral. Add two short vertical lines to fill in the right side of the scissors.

9 Closely echo stitch the entire motif.

Tomato Pincushion

The pincushion motif is stitched just like the Perfect Pumpkin (page 102) but with a different top. Stitch it on red fabric to re-create the tomato look.

1 Draw two parallel guidelines. Beginning just above the bottom line, stitch a letter *C*.

2 Stitch a shallow *C* back to the bottom guideline.

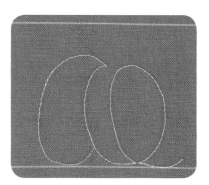

3 Stitch a clockwise oval.

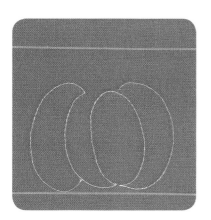

4 Add a backward *C*.

5 Add five to six narrow triangles on the top of the tomato.

6 Add pins by stitching short vertical lines with two to three stitches on top. Stitch over the vertical lines to begin another pin.

7 Stitch the right side of the tomato by starting a backward *C*.

8 One-third of the way down, stitch up to the top line at an angle, then make a loop.

9 At the top of the loop, stitch a looping swirl. Overstitch the swirl, then stitch down to finish the needle.

10 Curve down to complete the right side of the tomato, then swirl right to either end with a curlicue knot (page 26) or begin the next motif.

Practice drawing designs here.

xxxxxxxxxxxxxxxxxxxxxxxxxxxxxxxxxxxxxxxx

Needle and Thread

Complete your basket of sewing notions with my favorite, the Needle and Thread. Combine it with Spools of Thread (page 119) and the Tomato Pincushion (page 116) for a fabulous border or background.

1 Stitch a small oval counterclockwise.

2 Add a short, straight line.

3 Stitch a line back to the tip of the oval and add a loopy thread tail to begin the next motif.

Spools of Thread

The Spools of Thread motif is the perfect addition to any quilt. Create a variety of spool shapes and thread embellishments for a spectacular border or background fill. Consider ending a row of spools with a Needle and Thread (page 118) as shown here.

1 Draw two parallel guidelines. Stitch from the bottom line to the top line. Stitch an angled line, then a horizontal line to the right. Angle back down to the top line.

2 Stitch from right to left along the top guideline. Closely echo stitch back.

3 Stitch a vertical line down to the bottom guideline. Stitch from right to left on the guideline. Echo stitch back to the right.

4 Stitch a short angled line, a horizontal line, and another angled line to complete the spool.

5 Add any decorative stitch to fill the spool, then add a loop thread tail to begin the next motif in the row.

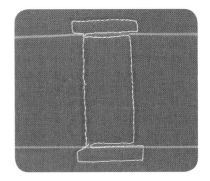

6 Add variety by stitching straight rather than angled spool ends and changing decorative elements within each spool, as shown at the top of this page.

Dog Bones

Quilt your faithful dog a bone with this easy motif. Add a loopy line to connect the bones as a background fill or border.

1a Starting at the bottom, stitch two deep scallops up and to the right.

1b Add a short, straight line.

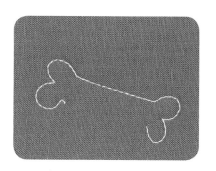

1c Stitch two more deep scallops.

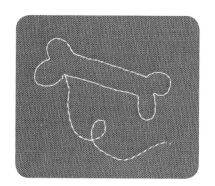

1d Complete the bone with a short, straight line, parallel to the first line. Add a loopy line to begin the next motif.

2 Add your dog's voice with words like *bow wow, woof, ruff,* or *arf.*

Little Kitty

Add a tabby or two to your next quilt with this whimsical motif. Stitch a single motif in the center of all the quilt blocks, or add it to your signature as your trademark.

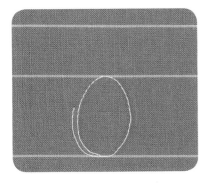

1 Draw three parallel guidelines. The upper space should be about half as big as the lower space. Beginning on the baseline, stitch a clockwise oval. Closely echo stitch the left side.

2 Add a counterclockwise circle.

3 Closely echo stitch the right side of the head, adding two small triangle ears on top.

4 Take a few stitches along the left side of the circle. Stitch an angled line out and overstitch back and into the center of the circle.

5 Add five more overstitched lines to create the whiskers. Overstitch back to the right side of the kitty's head.

6 Closely echo stitch the right side of the body and add a tail.

Circus Train

Trains are the perfect addition to a little boy's quilt or to holiday quilts. Add smoke coming out of the engine and fill the train cars with quilted surprises. Choose messy, silly, or basic spirals (page 18) for the train tires.

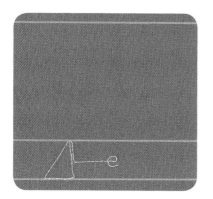

1a Draw three lines. From the middle line, stitch down, left, and up to make a triangle. Stitch halfway down the right side, add a horizontal line, and begin a spiral.

1b Complete the first spiral on the right side. Add a horizontal line and stitch a second spiral, again ending on the right side of the spiral.

1c Echo stitch above the tires to the front triangle. Stitch a short vertical line, and stitch over four or five stitches.

1d Add a small triangle for a smokestack. Stitch to the right a few more stitches. Stitch a short vertical line.

1e Add a narrow rectangle for the roof.

1f Stitch a rectangle to make a window, then down and to the right to begin the next motif.

$2a$ To begin a coal car, draw three parallel lines. Stitch two spirals, ending on the right side.

$2b$ Echo stitch above the top of the spirals. Stitch a slightly angled line.

$2c$ Add a narrow rectangle on the top. Extend the rectangle slightly beyond the width of the tires.

$2d$ Add an embellishment to the side of the train car, ending on top, just below the narrow rectangle. Complete the train car by stitching a line angled toward the wheels.

$2e$ To fill a long border, stitch multiple coal cars. Vary the decorations or personalize the cars with names or phrases.

$3a$ To begin the caboose, stitch two spiral wheels. Echo stitch back to the left side.

$3b$ Stitch a small bumper over the wheel and add a vertical line upward. Stitch a narrow rectangle.

$3c$ Add a decoration to the roof by stitching a smaller rectangle.

3d Stitch from right to left to complete the decoration. Stitch right, down, and then left for the roof.

3e Drop down and add two windows, ending below the roof. Take two stitches to the right and then down and two stitches to the right again.

3f Stitch down to complete the back bumper and then spiral upward, ending with a curlicue. Overstitch the curlicue to secure.

Practice drawing designs here.

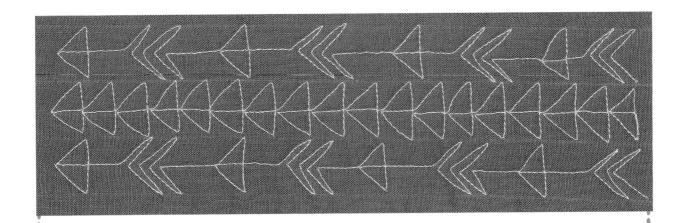

Backgrounds and Fills

Backgrounds and fills are the mainstays of the quilter's toolbox. Learn a wide variety of background motifs to add just the right touch to all of your quilts. Choose from modern motifs like Chevrons and Arrows (page 138) and Woodgrain (page 137) or whimsical patterns like Silly Spirals (page 126). Most background motifs are easily modified to fill a border or a single block. Beginners should start with Honeycomb (page 134). More advanced quilters might like Deirdre's Diamonds (page 130) and Water and Ice (page 136).

Silly Spirals

There are many ways to stitch spirals. Silly Spirals add a modern whimsical appeal. Stitch rows of Silly Spirals or change directions and fill a grid.

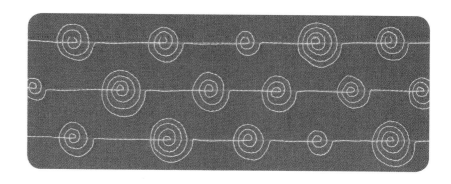

1 Stitch a straight line. At the end of the line, stitch upward at an angle to begin the center of the spiral.

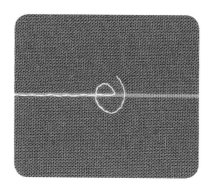

2 Continue stitching counterclockwise.

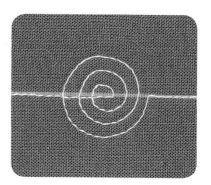

3 Stitch evenly spaced circles to create a spiral. End the spiral on the line, on the side from which you want to proceed. Stitch along the line to begin the next motif.

4 Stitch rows of silly spirals where the spirals are offset, as shown above, or draw a grid and add spirals in a variety of sizes to create a very modern background.

Sticks and Stones

Sticks and Stones is a very modern border or background pattern. Use a ruler or stencil to draw a grid. I used a Square Grid Stencil (SCL-455-12) from the Stencil Company. The stencil is a 1" grid. I marked every other line to create a 2" grid. For marking, a Clover chalk wheel rolls over the grid easily. Instead of a circle, stitch any spiral for a fun variation.

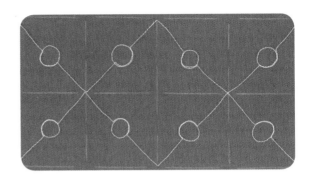

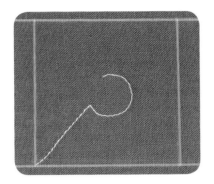

1 Beginning in the lower-left corner, stitch a short diagonal line upward, ending slightly before the center of the square. Stitch a circle.

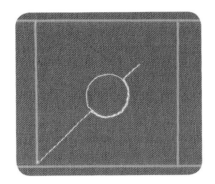

2 Stitch 1½ times around the circle and then stitch a straight diagonal line to the upper-right corner.

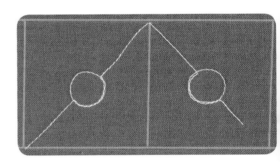

3 Stitch a short diagonal line downward and add a circle in the center as before. Stitch down to the bottom-right corner.

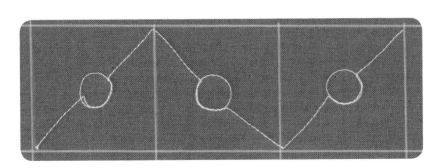

4 Continue zigzagging up and down to fill a border.

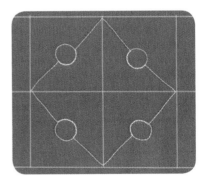

5 To stitch a single block or a border square, form an on-point square of Sticks and Stones.

Loose Screws

Loose Screws is a more fluid version of Silly Spirals (page 126). Stitch it in rows or clusters as an allover motif in place of meandering.

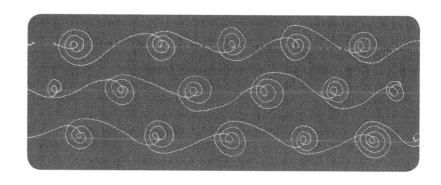

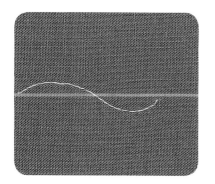

1a Draw a guideline. Stitch a shallow *S* wave, curving first above and then below the guideline.

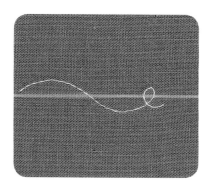

1b Add a counterclockwise loop over the line.

1c Continue spiraling in evenly spaced circles around the loop, and then add another Loose Screw in any direction.

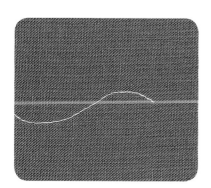

2a To make a reverse spiral, stitch an *S* wave that first curves downward.

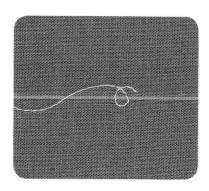

2b Stitch a clockwise loop over the line.

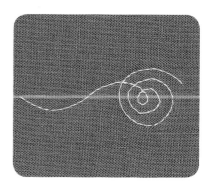

2c Spiral in evenly spaced circles around the loop.

Moon and Stars

Moon and Stars is one of my favorite background motifs because it's easy to stitch. Any time you get stuck in a corner, echo stitch to a new area. Try glow-in-the-dark thread for a true night sky effect!

1 Beginning anywhere on the quilt, stitch a small letter *C*. Echo stitch one or two times.

2 Add triangles around the center.

3 Add another echo-stitched half circle.

4 Add as many triangles as required to travel around the center. Stitch another half moon. Echo stitch two or three times.

5 Continue adding half moons and triangles to fill the background.

Deirdre's Diamonds

Diamonds are a versatile motif that can be stretched and pulled for different effects. Stitch long, thin diamonds for a dramatic Harlequin design, or combine large and small diamonds to create the Argyle pattern.

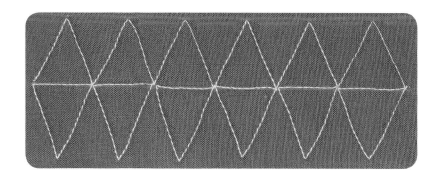

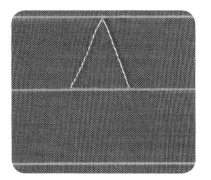

1a Draw three evenly spaced parallel guidelines. Beginning on the centerline, stitch the top of a triangle.

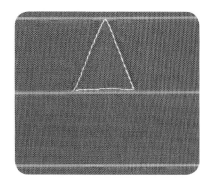

1b Stitch on the centerline back to the first stitch.

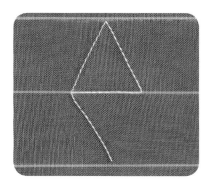

1c Stitch at an angle to the bottom guideline.

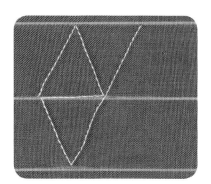

1d Stitch a long diagonal line through the centerline to the top guideline. This line should be parallel to the first diagonal line.

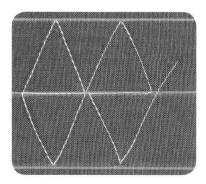

1e Stitch at an angle to the centerline. Stitch from right to left on the centerline. Stitch an angled line to the bottom guideline. Stitch the long diagonal line through the center to continue the next diamond.

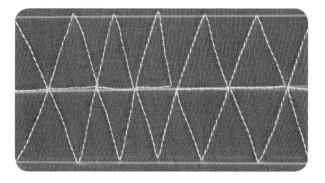

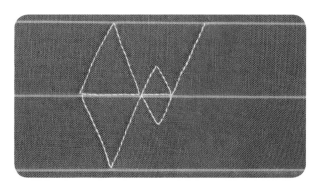

2 Vary the spacing to create different looks. Notice only the width of the diamonds has changed. The angled lines are still parallel to each other.

3a Add a small diamond after each large diamond.

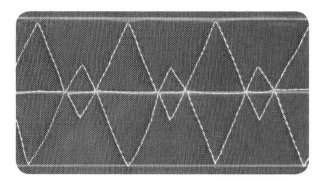

3b Stitch different variations of Deirdre's Diamonds within a single quilt to create interesting textures.

Practice drawing designs here.

Zigzags and Rickrack

Zigzags are a classic element that can be modified to embellish any style of quilt.

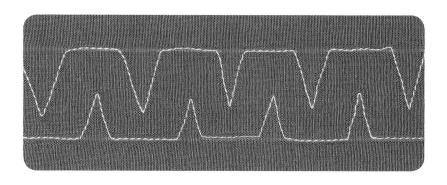

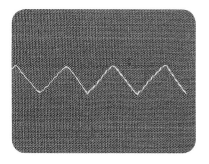

1a Quilt a simple zigzag to create a whimsical hand-drawn element, perfect for Halloween quilts.

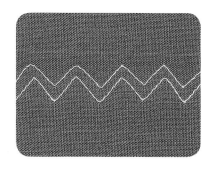

1b Echo stitch the zigzag to create Rickrack, an adorable pattern for children's quilts.

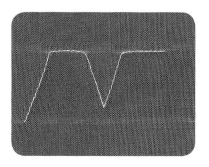

2a For a Zigzag motif, draw two parallel guidelines. From the bottom line, stitch at an angle to the top. Add a short horizontal line to the right. Stitch the letter *V* and then a short straight line to the right.

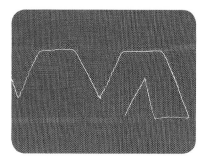

2b Continue adding *V*s and horizontal lines to complete a row. At the end of the row, stitch to the bottom line. Add a short horizontal line and upside-down *V*.

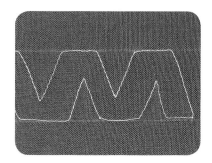

2c Continue adding horizontal lines and upside-down *V*s to complete a row.

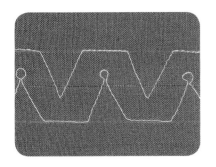

3a The Embellished Zigzag adds another dimension to the Zigzag. Add a small circle to the upside-down *Vs* while stitching the bottom row.

Wrap It Up with Rickrack

When you're quilting a wholecloth quilt with many different motifs, it helps to corral all those different designs. Consider framing your quilt with a simple Rickrack border, as shown in Scissors on page 141, Halloween Sampler on page 142, and Notions on page 143.

Practice drawing designs here.

Honeycomb

The Honeycomb is a versatile and easy background fill. It can be stitched very small or very large by adjusting the spacing between the lines.

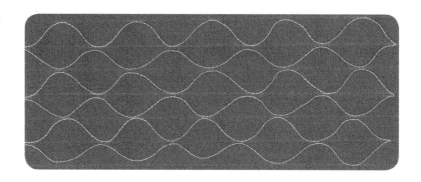

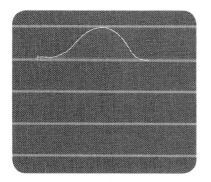

1 Draw several parallel guidelines. Beginning on the line below the top guideline, stitch a tapered scallop.

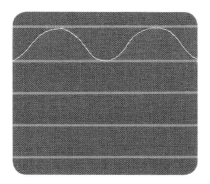

2 Add as many tapered scallops as needed to fill the background.

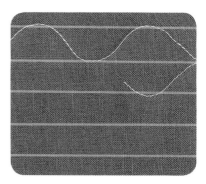

3 At the end of each row, reverse direction and stitch upside-down tapered scallops down to the third line, mirror-imaging the scallop above.

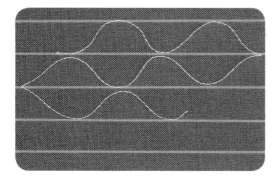

4 End each row on a downward taper. Reverse direction and begin the next row of tapered scallops to reveal the Honeycomb design.

Wavy Lines

Sometimes simple is best. Wavy lines are easy to free-motion quilt, and they can be combined with other motifs or aligned in interesting patterns to fill any quilt or block quickly.

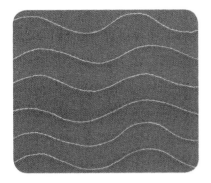

Simple, evenly spaced wavy lines can be used to fill a single block or stitched across an entire quilt.

Include a simple element like a circle to add variety and a modern touch to the wavy line.

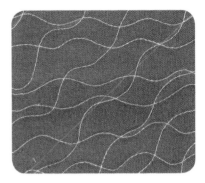

For a watery look, stitch parallel rows of wavy lines and then add diagonal wavy lines on top.

Create movement and texture with wavy lines by stitching them in different directions across the quilt or within a block.

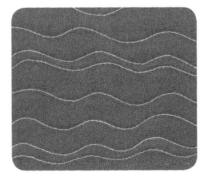

Change the look by stitching wavy lines at varying distances from each other.

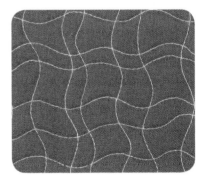

Overlap wavy lines to create a simple grid.

Water and Ice

This modern motif adds a pretty texture to any quilt. When stitched diagonally across a quilt, the swirly pattern resembles water or ice.

1 Begin by outlining the area to be quilted. Draw a diagonal line across the outlined area.

2 Beginning in the upper-left corner, stitch a wavy line along the diagonal line and then curl back to the left.

3 Swirl back out to the right and extend another wavy line beyond the first swirl. Roughly follow the drawn diagonal line.

4 Continue adding loose swirls across the quilt. At the end of the row, stitch back to the beginning by very loosely echo stitching above the swirls.

5 Begin another row of watery swirls and continue adding rows of swirls and loose echo stitching to fill the area.

Woodgrain

The beautiful lines found in wood create a modern texture for any quilt. This easy motif is a great substitute for meandering or stippling on many quilts. I first learned this motif from Molly Hanson's *Free-Motion Quilting for Beginners* (Martingale, 2014), which includes this and other motifs.

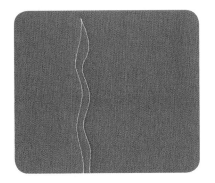

1 Stitch a vertical wavy line. Echo stitch back to where you started.

2 Add a shorter echo-stitched wavy line.

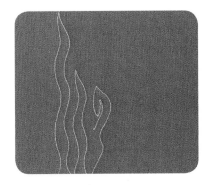

3 For the third row, begin the wavy line and stitch downward to begin a knot, shown in the next step.

4 To create the knot, stitch a tapered scallop and spiral in to the center.

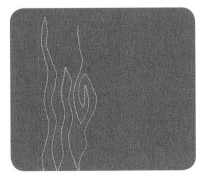

5 Spiral out of the knot and extend the wavy line upward.

6 Fill in the gap with another knot or short wavy lines. Continue filling the background with echo stitching, wavy lines, and knots.

Chevrons and Arrows

This simple motif adds a modern element to any quilt. Stitch a single row of Chevrons and Arrows for a quick border or combine rows to create a background. Cover an entire quilt by stitching the pattern from edge to edge.

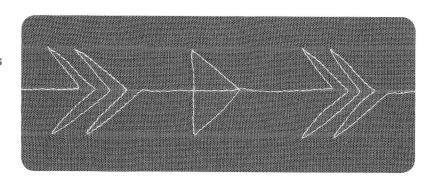

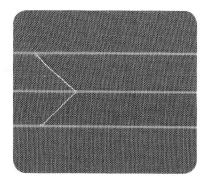

1 Draw three evenly spaced parallel guidelines. Begin stitching on the top line. Create a chevron by stitching an open triangle to the centerline and then down to the lower guideline.

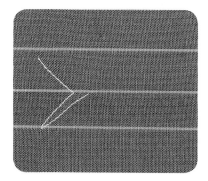

2 Closely echo stitch to the centerline.

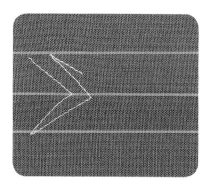

3 Echo stitch to the top guideline and then start stitching down toward the centerline.

4 Continue adding echo stitching for several stitches then stitch to the right along the centerline.

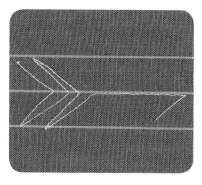

5 To begin the arrow, stitch at an angle downward to the lower line.

6 Stitch a vertical line to the top line. Stitch to the centerline to close the triangle and complete the motif. Stitch right along the centerline to begin the next motif.

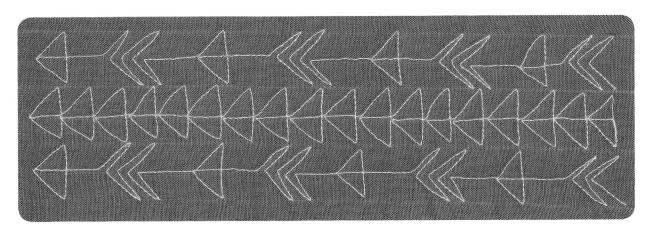

7 Combine rows of the motifs to create different patterns and add variety to your quilt.

Practice drawing designs here.

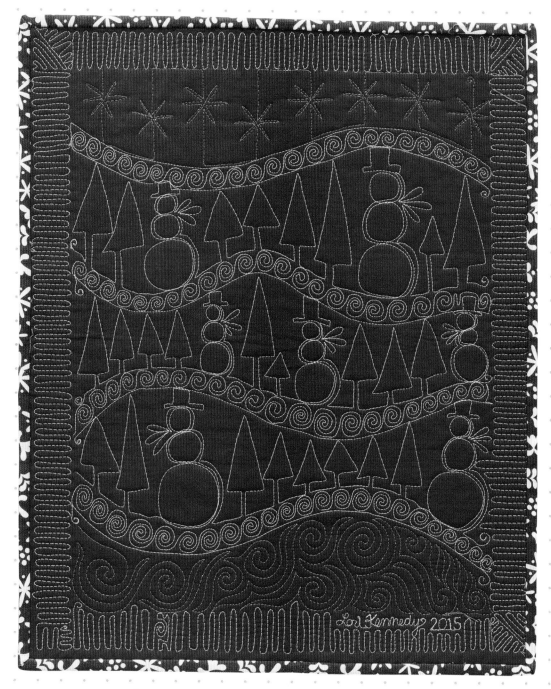

Winter Wonderland uses the following motifs:
Snowballs and Snowflakes variation (page 42)
Mr. Snowman (page 45)

Scissors uses the following motifs:
Sewing Scissors (page 114)
Zigzags and Rickrack (page 132)

Holly uses the following motifs:
Holly and Berries (page 46)
Snowballs and Snowflakes (page 42)

Halloween Sampler uses the following motifs:

Moon and Stars (page 129)

Bats (instructions aren't in this book, but you
can easily free-form stitch your bats)

Silly Spirals (page 126)

Spiderweb (page 94)

Jack-o-Lantern (page 86)

Spooky Fence (page 92)

Spooky Spider (page 101)

Notions uses the following motifs:
Needle and Thread (page 118)
Spools of Thread (page 119)
Sewing Scissors (page 114)
Tomato Pincushion (page 116)
Zigzags and Rickrack (page 132)

Poinsettia Tic-Tac-Toe uses the following motifs:
Perfect Poinsettia (page 38)
Candy Cane Border (page 39)